Praise for *Lay Pastoral Care*

"In *Lay Pastoral Care: A Narrative Approach*, Christie Cozad Neuger and Joretta Marshall use the narrative method to offer parish pastors a unique resource for reinvigorating laypeople's participation in congregational pastoral care. Drawing upon the insights of narrative therapy theory and collaborative learning, they create a model for training and overseeing lay caregiver networks that is guaranteed to stimulate and maintain interest and greater participation in the ministry of congregational pastoral care. This approach will be life-giving and sustaining for both care companions and care seekers. As a seminary professor who teaches on lay pastoral care, I believe this book is a must-read."

—Raynard D. Smith, associate professor of pastoral care/pastoral theology, New Brunswick Theological Seminary

"Joretta Marshall and Christie Cozad Neuger have written a timely book. In consideration of current traumatic experiences and continual grief and loss, they recognize that the work of caring for God's people cannot be done alone. They write with passion, using the lens of narrative theory and conveying deep understanding of the spiritual significance of community engagement in the care of souls. Consistent with the narrative approach to communal care long used in African American pastoral care, Marshall and Neuger foster new understandings of collaborative learning communities. The authors provide practical tools and rituals that can be used in a variety of congregational and community settings. They recognize that lay spiritual caregiving is at the heart of the church. Partnering is important. Reciprocal involvement with congregational leaders and parishioners is essential. But more important, lay involvement is crucial, and educating and equipping laypersons is vital. This book is indeed needed—for such a time as this."

—Beverly R. Wallace, coauthor of *African American Grief*, associate professor of congregational and community care, Luther Seminary, St. Paul, Minnesota

"After contributing to pastoral care literature over many decades, Marshall and Neuger offer another exciting collaboration. Their new book on narrative lay pastoral care belongs in all pastoral care conversations in seminary classrooms, church lay leader trainings, and communities of faith seeking mutual support in a world that needs healing."

—Mindy McGarrah Sharp, associate professor of practical theology and pastoral care, Columbia Theological Seminary, and author of *Creating Resistances: Pastoral Care in a Postcolonial World* (Brill, 2019) and *Misunderstanding Stories: Toward a Postcolonial Pastoral Care* (Pickwick, 2013)

"In these days of recovery from the unprecedented psychic stress of a global pandemic and the many isolations and adaptations it has required of us all, combined with the spiraling demands for mental health services in a society longing for healing from divisions, the wisdom and experience Marshall and Neuger bring to the conversation about culturally competent and spiritually relevant pastoral care for our time is needed now more than ever. Their reflections speak to our human condition and our need for coherence, connection, and hope."

—Deb Patterson, United Church of Christ pastor, member of the Oregon State Senate, and author of *The Essential Parish Nurse: ABCs for Congregational Health Ministry* (Pilgrim, 2003)

"Deeply grounded in the authors' experiences developing and nurturing lay pastoral care ministry, *Lay Pastoral Care: A Narrative Approach* is a must-read book for anyone who is committed to cocreating life-giving networks of care in congregations. The most profound value of this book, which is rich in practical resources and tools, is the clarity of the theological and psychological convictions that situate lay pastoral care in the mission of the church. The text is animated by the authors' down-to-earth descriptions of the attitudes and choices that enable diverse expressions of lay pastoral-care networks to grow and thrive. I hope this book will be required reading for all who are responsible to equip the priesthood of all believers for ministries of care in the congregation and in the world."

—Kathleen D. (Kadi) Billman, John H. Tietjen Professor of Pastoral Ministry: Pastoral Theology, emerita, Lutheran School of Theology at Chicago

"Through all the years I have trained laypeople in the skills of pastoral care, this is the training resource I've been searching for! Rich in narrative theory, yet approachable to anyone wishing to develop their caring abilities, this book promises to transform congregations through a consultative empowerment model of care that relies on the strengths and gifts of every person. It will be a welcomed gift to any community desiring to mobilize its members in skillful, caring response to the many precarities and vulnerabilities we face. I am eager to introduce this book to my own communities!"

—Cody J. Sanders, American Baptist chaplain to Harvard University and author of *A Brief Guide to Ministry with LGBTQIA Youth*

"A gentle, wise, and generative book. It provides a practical way to nurture and sustain profound connections among congregants and in the broader community. Neuger and Marshall place laypeople at the heart of ministries of care, providing concrete resources for those who value empowering, collaborative relationships. An instant classic."

—Duane R. Bidwell, professor of spiritual care and counseling, Claremont School of Theology

Lay Pastoral Care

LAY PASTORAL CARE

A Narrative Approach

Joretta L. Marshall

Christie Cozad Neuger

FORTRESS PRESS

MINNEAPOLIS

LAY PASTORAL CARE
A Narrative Approach

Cover Design: LUCAS Art & Design, Jenison, MI
Cover Art: Unsplash / Usgs / Daniele Levis Pelusi

Print ISBN: 978-1-5064-7450-2
eBook ISBN: 978-1-5064-7451-9

To Win with gratitude for the love, support, and partnership we have shared since we were teenagers and to our children, Dan (Chrissy) and Cathy (Gregg), who have extended our family so beautifully. And to Grace, Thomas, Casey, Gabby, and Kate, who give me such hope for the future. (Christie)

To Joy (my partner), whose love throughout the years has nurtured my spirit and life, and to Dana (my sister), who supported this work by taking care of household details while I focused on writing, editing, and Zoom sessions. (Joretta)

Contents

PREFACE

One aspect of the vocational journey that both of us have found meaningful over our professional lives has been that of teaching pastoral care. We have worked with students, institutions, congregations, communities, and denominations, encouraging each to reflect more deeply on what it looks like to companion people through very diverse moments in their lives and to educate others in the art of care. As we began the process of thinking about this book, we each took time to reflect on why this project is important to us and why we wanted to spend time writing a book together.

REFLECTIONS FROM JORETTA MARSHALL

There was only one church in the rural southwest Wisconsin community in which I grew up, and it happened to be a United Methodist congregation. I grew up with the people of that church being the center of my world in this small town. They nurtured me in the faith, they (or mostly my mom) taught me in Sunday school and later convened our youth fellowship, they encouraged me to go to seminary, they sat with my family when we needed extra support because of deaths or the general challenges of life, and they sent me forward into the world. We shared the pastor of this small church with two other neighboring communities. The pastors entered and left the community fairly routinely, either appointed by the bishop to other larger churches or headed toward retirement. Our church was one of those "stepping-stones" for pastoral leaders, which is not in any way a judgment on these folks. What is true is that while the pastors were with us, they generally did the best they could to show up for the people of the three churches they served. Some were more skilled in pastoral care, while others were best at offering thoughts and prayers.

It was in this community that I learned the most about the extension of God's love and grace through acts of pastoral care. Some of the teaching and learning came through the embodiment of care in a good pastoral leader who moved into the community. But more often, the real everyday care came in the form of casseroles delivered to our doorstep during a significant loss, in the prayers and tears of friends from the church who were as confused as we were by the presence of mental illness in our family, in the power of showing up at a local farmer's to help with chores and harvesting when tragedy struck their family, and in the celebration of the rituals of confirmation, graduation, and sending forth. The local people of that community did the best they could to offer care and extend the grace of God in everyday moments.

Over the years, I have remained grateful for the gifts of this faith community to me and to our family. I remember wondering as a child where it was that these ordinary folks learned how to care as part of their everyday lives. These kinds of questions led me to pursue ministry and to later teach in seminaries. What I have come to realize is that my community learned how to care from other laity who nurtured them every day and who taught them the gifts of hospitality, comfort, sustenance, and guidance as part of their faith journey. And from time to time, there was a good pastoral mentor who modeled healthy care in the life of the congregation. While the church was not great at every aspect of pastoral care, they were present in times of notable need.

What the local church often missed in its activities of pastoral care was an opportunity to articulate how theology and their offering of care reflected their understanding of God's love. In my community, we did not always know how to talk about challenging and difficult topics like gender identity, sexual orientation, or race. We did not always know how to respond to mental illness without implying that somehow there was a problem in a family, that God was trying to teach someone a lesson, or that if the right prayers were offered, someone would be saved from the vicissitudes of life. We did not always grasp the importance of helping people live into hope when despair seemed much more prevalent and real. Nor did we easily connect some of the larger social challenges of people in our community—such as farmers who lost their land and way of being in the midst of the farm crisis of the 1970s and '80s and who were more likely to find ways to end their lives—with our narratives of the gospel. And yet, this community of faith provided enough grace for me to learn something more intentionally about good pastoral care.

Many of the commitments that were shaped in me at an early age continue in different forms today. I still believe that the best pastoral care is an activity of the whole church and not something that is offered only by the ordained leader of a congregation. As the community walks with people over time, they become the caregivers and are the recipients of genuine acts of compassion, love, and concern. I learned much about the nuances and challenges of mental illness as a child and about the importance of people who walked the journey with my family, and today, I also know that there are some better ways to respond than how some well-intentioned church members did in those early days. Their hearts and spirits were in a place of genuine care, but their theologies and words weren't always life-giving. I needed a concrete reminder that there are some things we just do not understand in the world, and I found myself disturbed at the packaged responses that often spoke more about judgment than the grace of God.

My work on this project arises from the very core of these earliest experiences and from my theological conviction that God is at work in the everyday ministries of ordinary people who offer extraordinary care through presence, listening, and response. To offer the most faithful acts of care, congregations deserve to have opportunities to hone their skills and craft their ministries. Skilled pastoral care communities are gifts to the people of God. Members of faith communities can think carefully and deliberately about how to be helpful in walking with people on journeys, how to sit with others through suffering and in death, how to celebrate rituals of life and faith in holy moments, and how to be a companion over time. They deserve to be supported by one another as they reach out and make mistakes and refashion a theology that makes more sense for the care they want to offer. Congregations that have rich opportunities to grow in faith, to hone skills, to develop theologies, to be in conversation about ethical issues and the need for care of self and soul, and to learn from and with one another about God's vision of shalom for the church can change the world through their presence. Deeper theological reflection that informs care is a contribution to the church and all of its ministries.

Reflections from Christie Neuger

When I was a young mother, just having graduated from college and unsure of where I was headed, I experienced the onset of panic attacks. They were debilitating and confusing. I had no name for the experience (what many today would call agoraphobia), and after a few months, I went to my pastor to ask for help. He had no idea how to understand my experience either, but he gave me a suggestion to "maybe stop thinking so much about yourself and your anxiety and go visit some people who need help in the parish." We were living in a small town, and there weren't many resources for older people, so I began to visit some of the elderly of the church. In particular, I remember visiting with Mabel. She had lost her eyesight, and nearing the end of life, she wanted to go through the letters she had saved and "organize them." So I read letters to Mabel. And as she began to review her life and make sense and meaning of those key events and relationships, I began to find a life of meaning in engaging in a relationship of pastoral care with her. I have generally thought of those months, of both anxiety and discovery, as my experience of being called to ordination. But as I reflect on it now, many years later, I recognize the power of lay ministry. It wasn't just preliminary to my discovering a vocation, but those moments together were transformative for both Mabel and me. We were church together, and the meaning-making we experienced, each in our own way, was sacred. In some real ways, that was the beginning of my deep commitment to lay pastoral care in the congregation.

When I began at Richfield United Methodist Church (UMC) as a congregational member, I had just retired from an almost thirty-year career as a professor of pastoral care. I had long been committed to the importance of teaching religious leaders to provide the best possible care and counseling that a generalist could to their congregants. But I had, over time, begun to realize that the real possibilities in pastoral care would come from creating caring congregations—training as many people as possible, at the depth and breadth of which they were capable and desirous of learning, to care for one another and to learn how to be cared for. As I was invited to participate in reenvisioning what pastoral care might look like in this congregation, I began to think about working to generate a highly trained congregation that would engage in effective pastoral care with one another in as many ways and contexts as we could imagine. This would take nothing away from the pastor's role as provider of appropriate counseling and care, as needed and appropriate, or from the visitation work of the parish nurse, but it would have a positive impact on raising the level of well-being in the congregation. And with an increased sense of well-being, congregants would be more likely to engage in the work of ministry outside the bounds of the church.

I continue to experiment with new models of lay pastoral care, focusing on the three commitments that emerged from my own experience as a lay caregiver, a teacher of future pastors, and a consultant for lay pastoral care ministries. First, lay pastoral care can be transformative for both the caregivers and the care receivers. Second, the more people that experience a calling to some form of pastoral care and are empowered to act on that call with training and ongoing consultation, the higher the senses of well-being and connection are in the congregation. And third, both the training and consultation of lay ministry participants need to be done in collaborative and imaginative ways, drawing on newer models of care. In this book, for example, we will be drawing on the philosophies of both collaborative and narrative therapies for the training work. For me, the work discussed in this book and in the parishes where I consult represents a full circle of my experience, and I am grateful to have the chance to explore it here.

Acknowledgments

This book reflects the lived experiences of the staff and volunteers at Richfield UMC in Minnesota. We carry deep appreciation for their commitments, their engagement with narrative thinking, their willingness to learn with and from one another, and their spirit of care. This book would not have been possible without them. We would especially like to name, with gratitude, Kay Bergeland, the coordinator of lay pastoral care ministries at Richfield UMC.

Second, we give thanks for the wisdom and support of our editor, Rev. Dr. Beth Gaede. This project is better because of her commitments, knowledge, and gifts.

Finally, we acknowledge the deep respect and care that we (Christie and Joretta) have for each other. We have been longstanding colleagues who value each other's gifts of intellect and spirit. More importantly, our friendship represents not only our commitments to the field of pastoral care and congregations but also our deep appreciation of each other.

1

Lay Pastoral Care at the Heart of the Church

Brad is a member of Community Church in a midsized town in the Midwest. Over the last three years, he has been involved in a learning community that meets once a month with others who are invited to be "companions" for those in the congregation who need supportive pastoral care. During the past eight months, Brad walked with Peter, who was living with a recurrence of pancreatic cancer and the often painful season of treatments that seemed not to work. Peter and Brad had many conversations about his illness, his family, and his faith. Brad will never forget the conversation they had as Peter was discerning whether to suspend further treatments, both of them knowing that such a decision would signal a shift in living and dying. Peter's family—including Sharon, his wife, and their three adult sons and their families—began to see Brad as someone important to Peter's journey as well as to their own life as a family. Two weeks ago, Peter transitioned from life on this earth, and Brad sat with Sharon and their adult children throughout the last day of the journey. Brad has stayed in touch with the family while also inviting others in the congregation to step in during this season of loss and grief.

Community Church plans for the multilayered needs of their members by intentionally developing and training networks within the congregation that are focused on different aspects of care. During the walk with Peter over the last several months, Brad was able to contact those on the food team to assist the family when prepared meals were welcomed. Prayer shawls were created by another team and offered to Peter and Sharon, allowing them to literally feel the care of Community Church when they sat in the hospital, the treatment center, or at home. After Peter's death, others from the congregation intentionally attended to the family through the immediate loss and ongoing work of grief. Rev. Shelby, the pastor of Community Church, reached out to plan for the rituals that accompany life and death, contributing specific wisdom and support.

While Brad will stay in touch with the family, he also trusts that others are ready to pick up with offering care in the days and months to come. Brad is relieved to know that a larger network of care functions within the church, with each member who is part of these networks participating in an ongoing learning community where they develop skills, process their experiences, and coconstruct their theologies. The various members of the network reflect intentionally on what their offering of care represents to themselves and to the community, and they are ready to step in to address specific needs.

As Brad begins to process the experience of the last year and the intensity of the last few months, he spends time with Phyllis, another layperson who coordinates the caring ministry networks within Community Church. Together, they remember that joining others in the profound journey of illness, suffering, and death has a reciprocal impact on one's spiritual life and on their relationships. While the conversation with Phyllis did not answer any of the complex questions that Brad seemed to have about whether he offered enough care to Peter or whether it was helpful, or about how Peter's illness seemed to return so quickly and how angry Brad was at the devastation it had on Peter's health, it was clear to them that their mutual relationship made a difference for both of their spiritual journeys. Brad realizes how the time with Peter created a new awareness in him about the steadfastness of God's presence, even while raising questions about why suffering is so present in the world around him. Peter and Brad forged a spiritual friendship that was filled with theological conversation and reflection, some of which had no obvious resolution. Toward the end of the conversation with Phyllis, Brad remarked that his life has been deeply touched by his experience with Peter and his family. He finds his changing theology to be life-giving even when it is poignant and painful.

In their conversation, Phyllis and Brad note their gratitude for being part of a congregation that prepares its members to reach out and care in different ways and at different times. The multilayered networks of care at Community Church contribute to a deeper and more compassionate presence among the members of the congregation, many of whom are part of different ministries within the church. Their intentional training for specific tasks invites the whole community to bring their best gifts, trusting that others are present when they individually cannot be. In addition, they understand that their work together belongs to the church. They are not replacing the pastoral leadership, nor are they simply supplementing the work of care that the pastor offers. Instead, there is a deeper sense that the church itself is called to ministries of care with one another. While the impact on the individuals who participate in the various networks is transformative, it is also true that the identity of Community Church is changing through its experience of intentional training, collaborative learning communities, and the practices engaged by the networks of care.

Intentional Networks of Care

This vignette, while imaginary, is built around an actual congregation where networks of care have become one of the prominent features of the community. Pastoral care is best embodied in congregations where multiple groups focus on different aspects of need and care. Each group is intentionally trained to respond to particular situations, whether sitting with someone during a time of grief and loss, providing meals for families in crisis, or walking with another church member through a health crisis. Because the networks are multilayered, they can respond to a breadth of pastoral care needs, not simply to those who seem to be in the most need at any given moment. We know that congregational members' gifts of talents, time, and opportunities are diverse. Likewise, there is a rhythm to our collective work of care, as some people function at times as caregivers, while at other times, they are the ones in need of care. In networks of care, people are encouraged to offer the level of care ministry that meets their own life circumstances. Developing networks of care in congregations not only recognizes the multiple gifts and needs within a community of faith but also provides ongoing training in order for people to bring their best to the work of pastoral care. This book and the model we propose are designed to assist laypersons who want to be more effective partners in care with one another.

At the heart of effective pastoral care in every congregation, regardless of size, are laypersons who want to know how best to care for one another. The development of networks such as the ones identified in the opening story contributes not only to direct care with members but also to the larger vision and work of a congregation. While this is not a book on the nature of the church, it is impossible to focus on pastoral care without reflecting on how these networks enhance the church and its well-being. Four aspects of what it means to be the church in the world are enriched through the development and training of networks of care.

First, the model we propose builds on a basic reality in congregational life: Members have consistently been present in one another's lives at everyday levels for as long as the church has existed. Participants in church school classes care about one another—not always perfectly, but genuinely. They recognize the other children, youth, and adults in their groups, and they learn to value those around them in ways that allow them to feel connected to one another and to the congregation. It is not unusual for individuals or families moving through chaos to have basic needs met by other members of the congregation. Without being told what they should do, faithful friends show up to deliver casserole dishes, send cards, offer flowers, and make visits during times of need, tragedy, and grief. In rural communities, neighbors help one another bring in the crops or tend to the fields when a family needs assistance. Prayer chains and shawl ministries create ways of reaching out and connecting, offering tangible gifts in the middle of life journeys that are sometimes precarious and tender. Church members show up to rebuild houses after a hurricane, to feed the poor, or to protest the way that we treat one another because of racism, heterosexism, or nationalism. These all represent acts of care within communities of faith. At its best, the church is committed to transforming the world through love of God and neighbor, embodied in genuine acts of care.

Such care is central to communities of faith and to life. We see the needs of the world around us, and we hope that the church and those who represent it are prepared to offer care. Yet we are called to not only be caregivers; we are also recipients of care within these same communities. The divide between caregiver and care receiver disappears as we recognize that congregations are built around human beings who are not divided by strength and weakness or perfection and desperation; rather, communities of faith are filled with glimpses of human beings who are both vulnerable and strong, resilient and challenged. The church is not made up of people who are troubled and people without trials; it is, instead, filled with creatures who experience all of this. For example, in the previous case, while Brad is a companion at a time when Peter needed support, it is also true that Brad's mother died several years ago, and the church was there to respond to his own family's needs during their grief. Networks of care rely upon the strength and gifts of ordinary people to meet one another in the extraordinary moments of life.

Second, networks of care acknowledge that the church is a place to intentionally learn and grow. Education has always been central to the life of the community of faith. We gather to learn with and from one another, believing that such learning is central to the church's call in the world. Communities of faith that are intentional about teaching and learning organize these activities through church school classes, as well as formal and informal groups in a congregation's life. Often, the focus of these experiences is on the journey of faith, the meaning of the sacred text, the theology of a denomination, the connections between actions of justice and theological commitments, and other subjects of value in the church and among its members. Not only do local communities work in this way, but judicatory and denominational leaders also resource congregations through online programs, written materials, or teaching sessions. At the core of our commitments to lay training and pastoral care in this book rests the conviction that the church is strengthened as we empower laypersons to be agents of care within their congregation. As people have an opportunity to identify what is important to them and to grow in their capacities for theological reflection and action, they also reach out and educate others in ways that make a difference.

Some congregations experience the educational process as one that is "delivered" by experts or other individuals who have studied more than the rest of the community. The expert model sometimes unintentionally discourages others from taking leadership or bringing their best wisdom to the educational setting. In what follows, we assume that learning with and from one another is central to being the church. When learning takes place in a dynamic space where practices and theologies are questioned and challenged, deconstructed and coconstructed anew, then meaningful engagement and pastoral care can thrive.

This model values the multiple layers of care needed to reach out to individuals, families, groups, and communities. As witnessed by the opening case, Community Church has many ways to be involved with Peter and his family. Yet we have not always done a good job of training laypersons in the art of care, nor have we consistently reflected on diverse cultures and contexts of care. Similarly, we have not always addressed how systemic oppressions of racism or sexism or heterosexism or classism negatively impinge on individuals and families in our communities. We know that pastoral care is deeply connected to issues of justice, life-giving theologies, and adequate resources. The narrative approach we offer in this book brings a way to mobilize the values and resources of those seeking and offering care while, at the same time, deconstructing communal discourses that distort notions of justice. For example, as Brad discusses with Peter the possible ending of active treatment, questions about justice emerge in their conversation. Peter is worried about the financial burden his care has placed on his family because of a lack of insurance to offset treatment, and Brad is aware that the issues are deeper than just those related to Brad and his family. His own family has also faced some of these same questions about ongoing treatment for a family member who needs consistent dialysis. Justice-seeking care is significant in our approach in this book because we recognize that the issues that impinge on our daily living are often complex. The church is a stronger participant in the world when it explores these issues in thoughtful, critical, and engaged ways.

Third, our approach to care recognizes that laypersons are central to the work of the church and, more specifically, to pastoral care. While clergy have a role to play, good networks of care are not dependent on them alone. Nurturing and sustaining laypersons in their ministry with one another does not deny the importance of good pastoral leaders. However, because we believe that care belongs to the ministry of the whole church, what we propose here is neither clergy focused nor exclusively the property of those who are trained or ordained. Churches that imagine the care delivered by trained clergy persons to be better because they "know what to do" often miss the genuine gifts of laypersons who care for one another in everyday moments.

In this model, the term *pastoral* refers less to the status of someone in the church and more to the theological perspective one brings to the task of care. We believe that laypersons are the heart of congregational care. The intent of this book is to invite laypersons to reflect carefully on the multiple networks of care that they can be a part of in supporting and sustaining a community and to recognize the laity as fundamental to the pastoral care of the church. This book on lay pastoral care reflects the larger belief that all persons are children of God who both deserve care and bring gifts to offering care. The model we propose here relies upon the wisdom of laypersons while not denying the value of clergy and other professionals. The laity do not simply support the clergy or professional staff in pastoral care; rather, they bring gifts and graces to the tasks of care because of their life experiences, wisdom, and diverse theological perspectives.

In a similar way, every layperson is a theologian who offers care because they believe that they are called to do so and that caring for one another is part of their role as participants in the church. Networks of care both value laypersons and empower them to shape meaningful relationships with one another as they live into the call of the community of faith. Clergy and staff are called in turn to nurture and support these networks of care, joining together to contribute to the thriving of community. In the illustration earlier, Phyllis has taken leadership to organize and support the network of care of Community Church. The network expands the caring activities of the church and creates significant opportunities for people to be present with one another in meaningful ways.

Phyllis provides ongoing space for people to reflect on their activities of care, which suggests that her leadership is central. Yet she is not the only expert in the room. There are laypersons who join her in developing networks of care that sustain and empower the congregation.

Fourth, developing networks of care not only extends hospitality and compassion for those who "belong" to our congregations; it also invites greater involvement with the broader community. Training lay members to be present in ways that are compassionate, thoughtful, and life-giving changes a congregation's self-understanding, encouraging their values and commitments to extend into the world. Communities that empower the laity to reach out to one another look for appropriate avenues to also reach out to families who surround them, whether they are in distress because of mental health / illness or in some other moment of "quiet" despair due to family violence or the loneliness that accompanies loss, divorce, or sending one's children into the world. Outreach for the church takes on new meaning as people feel more adequately trained to respond to others both within and outside of the church doors. This training can also enhance the way that participants view and address their own life challenges.

The training of laypersons to function in various pastoral care networks creates a transformative theology for a community of faith. As the networks expand and more training is done across the congregation, the church itself takes on a new identity based on the values of generating wisdom with one another, asking questions of theology that offer new visions, and building on commitments to be the church in the world. The membership of the church is changed as they discover more robust tools for caring. Persistent and faithful training is less about teaching people "what to do" and more about engaging people in their commitments to stand with one another in a complex world. The more members within a community are involved in the diverse aspects of care and intentionally trained to be participants in these networks, the greater the church's impact not only on their own lives but on the life of the community that surrounds them. These networks become part of the formative shaping of congregational life.

As noted in our opening vignette, Community Church is shaping a particular identity that arises from the deep networks of people who are trained in the art of pastoral care while also engaging in theological reflection. These activities become a gift to the broader community as Community Church sees their role in the world to be more than simply offering care to one another. They extend the gifts of pastoral care into the work of every mission and ministry activity in the church.

Formative Practices of Care

Religious communities have always understood that part of their task is to shape faithful persons. We participate in practices of the church in hopes that they will enrich our spiritual lives. To be formed by our values and commitments offers us a centered way of approaching situations, providing a point of view or a stance that helps us navigate the world. Formation occurs through formal and informal activities such as worship, liturgy, and individual and corporate prayers as well as studying Scripture together, educating one another on theological commitments, and being together in community. The integration of these habits and rituals into our daily lives, in turn, shapes our interpretation, our perspective, and our way of being in the world. For many, Christian formation means learning about the values and commitments of the gospel and drawing on them as we develop our vision and respond to it with actions of faith.

Practices are formative, as they shape the way that we see things and approach situations. The everyday practices of care—such as listening, attending, and being present—invite us to reflect on the world or on our situations, to seek wisdom, or to ask new questions. The narrative practices discussed later in this book help us listen carefully and patiently to what people do and don't say, to ask questions thoughtfully, to ponder differences in understanding and perspectives, and to remain curious about what is meaningful in life and in faith. Experiences of pastoral care, both as receiver and giver, also help us reflect on what is most valuable to us and how we discern the future. The care we receive from others at important moments in our lives helps shape our self-understandings and our commitments. Congregations that encourage deeper care among their members reach inward and outward with a more abundant sense of compassion and empathy for others.

The intentional training of lay pastoral caregivers offers an opportunity to integrate practices that help them pay attention to what matters most in their lives and in the world around them. The model we propose here focuses on training, in part because we believe it can be formative for persons in any church and for the community as a whole. These are practices that every layperson can participate in. They are not designed primarily for clergy, nor are they reserved only for large congregations. Pastoral care embodies attitudes and stances of care that we believe need to be practiced, much like one would practice any other art or skill that is important to them to develop. Ultimately, forming pastoral care companions contributes to a life-giving theology and church.

As we will suggest quite often, the model we propose in this book is less focused on learning techniques and is more invested in the development of a collaborative and empowering stance toward others with whom we are engaged. In the context of this stance, we generate pastoral practices. Everyone can learn more effective ways of offering and receiving pastoral care by paying attention to the practices that follow. Learning about these practices and engaging in them critically and thoughtfully can shape the way we see the world and the tasks of ministry and pastoral care. These strategies ground much of the work of the chapters that follow and are built around some of the best practices in the field of pastoral care.

Presence

A first, formative practice in pastoral care is an embodied presence that is centered, responsive but not reactive, thoughtful, and deliberate. This statement may seem obvious. However, we know that practicing presence is more than a simplistic theology of "showing up and being there," although that is often the first and most significant step in learning about caregiving. The number of painful stories we hear about churches or pastoral care persons who don't show up in a crisis is astounding. To be fully present with someone suggests not only that we show up but that we are intentional about seeing the person with whom we are engaged as a unique individual who is a child of God. Everyone is connected to larger systems and communities, and they carry narratives that are both healing and problematic. A caring presence acknowledges that every individual is both strong and weak, vulnerable and full of agency, and that we all inhabit pasts, presents, and futures that are intermingled. Those who show up on behalf of a congregation also "represent" a God who shows up, who cries tears with us, or who celebrates with us. In addition, they represent the church that believes in the Holy One.

To be fully present is hard work. Through our presence, we communicate to the other person a deeper awareness of them and their commitments, hopes, and values. Our focus shifts from the problems the person describes to the resources and strengths they bring to this moment. Such offering of presence means putting aside other matters that are on our minds and listening fully to someone's narrative even when it seems too painful or messy to bear while allowing the hope of something beyond us to hold us together in a moment of unpredictable grace. We can nurture specific skills that more fully communicate that we are present, and we will talk about some of these in the following chapters.

Through our presence, we intentionally focus on what is meaningful to the other person rather than on our own thoughts and beliefs. We carry both deep compassion and empathy, knowing every person's story is unique and what we think or believe is of less importance. What is significant about presence is that we participate in meaningful exchanges that invite people to name what is important to them and to call upon those resources within themselves and the community. Such a stance of presence shapes our perspective on the work of pastoral care.

Affirming Agency by Listening and Responding

A second formative practice of pastoral care is affirming the agency of the other through thoughtful questions, listening deeply without judgment, and working to increase our sense of empathy. We suggest less focus on acquiring more tools for diagnosis or mastering quick phrases for responding to concerns and more focus on thoughtful questions and curiosity that invite greater wisdom from others. In the chapters that follow, you will hear more about the power of language and the gift of asking beautiful questions, inviting people to share in ways that are important to them rather than expecting or demanding that they share feelings or experiences in a particular way. Careful and thoughtful questions can activate the agency of an individual to decide whether they want to reserve something or risk saying more in the telling of their story. The invitation is freely given with no expectation of sharing more or less than what someone chooses.

We often hear about reflective listening in pastoral care, and it is indeed important. Listening with a sense of reflexivity is often understood to be hearing what someone has said and then responding to them in ways that acknowledge that they were heard. Such a tool is significant in the communication process. However, it is only one resource for signaling that we are listening deeply, although it is too often viewed as the only way to respond to someone's sharing of a concern. Instead, as we will talk about later, disciplined listening includes remaining connected and curious as we invite care companions to bear witness to care seeker's wisdom, vulnerability, and strength as they emerge in the telling and retelling of their stories. Such listening does more than invite speech from another. The power of a more disciplined and intentional approach to listening encourages people to speak about what is important to them. Refraining from judgment as people share narratives that are holy to them is central to the work of pastoral care.

Rarely do we have the "right response" that assists someone in addressing their needs and concerns. Crafting appropriate responses to what one hears is, in itself, an art. What we are suggesting here is not counseling, nor is it advice giving; rather, by inviting someone to retell a story, we encourage them to bring their best wisdom to their own lives. We are not present to solve problems with people; rather, we become companions and conversation partners as, together, we reflect on the hopes and values of the care seeker. There are no easy answers in disciplined listening. Likewise, there is no grand narrative or theory through which everything must be shaped. Careful and deep listening invites people to rich and potentially transformative dialogue. Pastoral care is not about being "smart" enough to let people know that you care, nor is it about figuring out what kind of question to ask so that you can confirm something you already suspect is true; rather, it is about listening deeply and learning with one another in unconventional ways about what is both important and valued by the care seeker.

The approach we suggest in this book is built around the insights of narrative therapy, where listening carefully to the narratives of people and inviting forth new ways of telling those narratives can be transformative not only to the care seeker but also to the one offering care. Such listening nurtures our ability to stand empathically with people in moments where there are no clear answers or responses. Empathy is a skill that requires the active participation of our intellect and discipline, our ability to connect with our emotions and those of others, and our openness to being with people in ways that change us relationally. Such disciplined listening reflects the theological commitment that there are far fewer right and wrong answers to people's most challenging questions than we sometimes wish. Much more will be said about this in the following chapters as we look at the power of narrative theory to shape our formative practices of care.

Theological Reflection

Good practices of care encourage thoughtful theological reflection. We know that people, in their daily lives, are already thinking theologically. Our language with one another, our observations about what we think and believe, and our interpretations of the world around us reveal deeply held beliefs about God, the nature of human beings, and the complexity of the world. Pastoral care always embodies theological assertions or assumptions. The way we make sense of the stories of our lives suggests that we are meaning-making people and that our faith is often an essential part of that process. The language of theology, however, does not have to be spoken in order for a conversation to be theologically reflective. Theology is often implicit in how we respond to one another or to the crises in our lives.

Training in pastoral care must invite people to not only name their theological assumptions but also reflect upon them in light of questions that emerge in caring with others. Pastoral care requires that we do not assume that what we have been taught in the past represents the ultimate truth for the present or the future. In a similar manner, effective pastoral caregivers are thoughtful about their own theological commitments, and they remain curious and open about their own belief systems. The most dangerous theology is one that unintentionally shows up in moments of distress or care and that assumes the truth of a belief that can be damaging or harmful to someone else. We draw upon theologies that are familiar to us when we sometimes don't know what else to say or how else to respond. For example, to suggest that God knows all things and will take care of all things or to assume that God will heal a particular illness or relationship in a specific way does not convey an openness to the spirit of God. Wrestling with our own theology in the company of others who are learning together how best to provide care allows us the space to work some things out in our thinking, avoiding the unintentional use of theology as a weapon or a defense in a critical moment of care. Holding our theology lightly, yet carefully, means we are less likely to overinterpret God's work or argue about what is the "right" stance or decision in a moment in time.

Effective pastoral care helps people reflect on who the Holy One is to caregivers and seekers as well as who we are as a community of faith. By thinking through our various faith claims, we encourage more intentional theological reflection in the congregation as a whole. Engaging in pastoral care with others inevitably generates and contributes to our deliberation about our faith. Developing opportunities for theological reflection in our training programs encourages this formative practice of care.

The Power of Collaborative Learning

Collaborative learning enhances the training and nurturing of pastoral care networks. We know that laypersons bring a wealth of knowledge, wisdom, courage, and care into congregations. They are the experts on how that community functions or how it gets in its own way. They don't all agree on what the answers or solutions are to the issues that surround them, but in general, they are eager to learn how to care more faithfully with one another. Developing, training, and nurturing laypersons in the art and skills of pastoral care can make a difference not only in an individual's life but also in the community.

Most definitions of the term *collaborative* refer to the way that we walk or work with one another. The definition that informs what follows is built around a model that encourages the creation of new understandings, new questions, and new visions of the world. Collaboration suggests more than people walking side by side with one another and having an exchange. People in collaborative relationships seek to understand, empathize, and care about one another even when they deeply disagree about something important. The goal of the conversation is important in collaborative work, for through it, we seek to build up one another and encourage one another to thrive.

We know that in our culture, not every conversation is designed to be collaborative. Debates, for example, are often built on models of arguing and defense, assuming there is a winner and a loser. People attempt to argue in a more convincing manner or to point out the holes in someone else's theory. In these situations, they are not genuinely engaged with one another out of a sense of curiosity or because they want to develop greater empathy. Instead, the goal for many people in debates or academic discourse is to win an argument or convince someone else about the certainty of their claim. Collaborative relationships are countercultural in the most profound way. Rather than following the cultural norms of winning and losing, collaborative work is built on a genuine valuing of one another's vision and expertise, gifts and graces, uniqueness and challenges.

Collaborative learning asserts that there is wisdom and deeper understanding when we learn from and with one another. In this model, there is less dependency on identifying who is the "teacher" and who is the "learner," believing instead that we learn with and from one another's journeys in ways that create something altogether new. This vision of training for lay pastoral care does not dismiss the expertise that someone with a background in counseling might bring to aspects of pastoral care; rather, it values the wisdom each person who is part of the network of care brings. In collaborative learning models, we wrestle with one another's ideas, speak openly and honestly, imagine and reimagine life-giving practices of care, and work toward the thriving of everyone in the community. Such learning communities become formative and transformative as people together face the complexity of caring for one another in the world around them.

Three values stand out in our claim that networks of care work best when they grow out of collaborative learning environments. The first value is something we have suggested all along in this chapter: each person brings gifts and graces, as well as vulnerabilities and challenges, to the task of pastoral care. The goal is not to teach someone to be a perfect caregiver or receiver; rather, the goal of collaborative learning is to bring our best selves to the work of pastoral care. Although not everyone is trained formally in care and counseling, we believe that each person brings something unique and important to the work of caregiving. Collaborative models deeply value the wisdom and expertise that is present in the room, knowing that we will be surprised by the gifts that emerge.

The second value is mutuality, which acknowledges that others have ideas and perspectives that we do not carry. Even when we might deeply disagree with someone, collaborative learning requires that we work to stand with one another and try to gain greater empathy—to understand who that other is, to be curious about their strengths, and to be willing to learn from them. These are important concepts in narrative and collaborative models and will be developed more in what follows.

Related to the importance of mutuality, we have struggled in this book with what language we should use for what has traditionally been called *caregiver* and *care receiver*. The notion of caregiving and care receiving implies a one-way relationship from an active caregiver to a passive care receiver. This stands against our commitments to mutuality. While there are times we do fall back into the term *caregiving*, we are attempting to use the more reciprocal language of *care companion* and *care seeker*. We have already asserted that *caregivers* and *care receivers* are not fixed positions. Sometimes one who has been a caregiver may well become a seeker in their own life crisis. Similarly, those in need of care at certain times in their lives can also be the ones who offer care to others. But even when they are temporarily in this giving-and-receiving relationship, it is more mutual than the traditional language implies. Mutuality does not imply equivalency of power, function, and responsibility. It does, however, imply the give-and-take of authentic relationships. We will talk more about this in a later chapter.

The third value is that something unique is created in our connection with one another. Collaborative therapy upholds the importance of joining with a person who is seeking care. This does not mean merging with care seekers or feeling their every emotion and experience; rather, joining with others suggests that one is open to being changed by another's presence. As people join with one another, they create a new relationship that has the potential to change them both. In addition, in collaborative work, such a process invites new reflections or new ways of imagining old things. For example, we might be open to exploring theologies as new questions emerge while we sit with someone who is experiencing a crisis in their life and recognize there are no easy answers. Indeed, something new is created in our connection with one another and in the networks of care that operate within a community of faith. Congregations are changed as they realize that their empathy for others and visions for justice have been deepened by pastoral care experiences. New questions, new reflections on theology, and an expanded awareness of the breadth of God's realm are nurtured in collaborative work. Ultimately, people in such mutual and collaborative learning communities feel more connected to one another and work to create space for all to thrive.

Networks of care are not only formative places for the development of practices of care; they are also collaborative learning environments where people can explore their commitments and their values, where they can struggle with theological concepts, and where they can genuinely be their best selves. The commitments and values of both collaborative and narrative theories offer life-giving ways to move forward in training those involved in a congregation's network of care.

The Focus of This Book

This book is designed for laypersons and those who are called to organize and/or train the networks of care within any size congregation. We believe that a multilayered approach to lay pastoral care can make a qualitative difference in the church and in communities of faith. These networks contribute to richer understandings of care with one another. In addition, people who engage in this model of care remain more curious, rather than absolute or directive, about why there are differences or about how someone approaches a particular situation.

This model assumes that care belongs to the community and not only to individuals, pastors, or professional staff. We assert that the greater the percentage of congregational members trained in any of the aspects of care, the greater the change to the community's identity and way of being in the world. When care is nurtured in this way, a congregation's self-understanding will shift. More questions about faith and theology will be asked, with less certainty about the answers. Our focus in this book is on empowering and enriching congregations through the development of lay caregiving networks. Our belief is that the development of a variety of trained and supported care groups will enrich the members of those groups, the care seekers to whom they minister, and the congregation as a whole. We have found that the philosophies and practices of both narrative and collaborative therapies provide a strong foundation for these kinds of care groups in both their training and their pastoral care work. The next three chapters will explore these ideas and practices.

A QUESTION TO CONSIDER: Why do the authors suggest lay pastoral care is "at the heart of the church," and why do they recommend congregations build intentional *networks* of care?

2

Presenting Narrative Therapy Theory

We have mentioned the idea of "narrative" several times already, including in the subtitle of this book, so we want to introduce some important ideas drawn from narrative therapy, an approach to counseling that focuses on inviting multiple stories in people's lives, not just the problem stories. We don't in any way want to imply that the material in this book, or lay pastoral care training, is intended to help people become counselors. As we stated in chapter 1, we even want to avoid the language of "counseling" in this work because of its implications of expertise, advice giving, and hierarchy as well as the professional training required to become a counselor. Nonetheless, narrative therapy serves as a philosophical and practical foundation in our approach to lay pastoral care. Narrative therapy, as will be explored later on, proposes that people make meaning in their lives through the narratives they hold about themselves and the narratives that others ascribe to them. It asserts that problematic stories have real effects on people's lives and that the work of counseling is to help people find and tell their stories in ways that empower them.

Both of us have spent much of our careers as professors of pastoral care searching for a theoretical foundation that would do several things. First, it would pay attention not just to individual and personal life stories but also to the context and culture in which those life stories take place. Second, the clinical theory would value the life stories of the people coming for care more than it values the culturally accepted stories of what it means to be "normal" or "healthy." In other words, the theory would make room for and respect a great diversity of human experience and identity and would trust "local knowledge," the personal experience and wisdom of help seekers. Third, this approach would value collaboration and mutuality between caregiver and care seeker while acknowledging the power differences that exist when someone seeks help from another person whom they assume has significant, relevant experience. At the same time, it would minimize the power differences by establishing careful boundaries in the care relationship and by trusting the experience of all of those in the room. The theory would favor a consultative and conversational model rather than a counseling model. Fourth, the theory would support values and commitments, even theologies, that are fundamental to caregiving in the church. Values like justice, empowerment, and optimism would either be built into the theory or be compatible with it.

This is a daunting list of requirements for a clinical theory that could support pastoral care in congregations, and we searched for many years to find an approach that would fit these essential criteria. In the early 1990s, a consultative clinical approach began to be developed, emerging primarily out of Australia and New Zealand, that offered tremendous potential, given the values and commitments that we have highlighted. It was called "narrative therapy," although the cofounders of it were not completely convinced that this was the most helpful name. It was effective, efficient, value rich, collaborative, and culturally alert. We became convinced that this approach held promise for the work of pastoral care, both professional and lay.[1]

In the rest of this chapter, we briefly describe how narrative therapy informs the work of lay caregiving as we imagine it. We try to give enough information about narrative theory's primary assertions without making this a book about narrative therapy itself. Our goal is to help readers more fully understand our recommendations about both teaching/learning methods and a specific approach to lay pastoral care programs in congregations.

What's in a Name?

Let's start with the name itself. Both the words *therapy* and *narrative* are problematic for the description of this approach and for the work of lay pastoral caregiving. First, the *therapy* part of the name. The cofounders, Michael White and David Epston, stated in their first book about narrative therapy that they wished they had named it narrative therapies because this approach should not be seen as a single or fixed way of helping people.[2] In addition, in our culture, the word *therapy* conveys a lot of assumptions about expertise, therapist and patient relationships, health and pathology, and the nature of helping conversations. These assumptions do not fit well with narrative therapy's much more consultative and collaborative nature.

Unfortunately, when describing this approach, we have to use the name *narrative therapy* in order to reference it accurately. Instead of thinking of this approach as a "therapy," however, it is more useful to think of it as a consultative model that relies on the experience, values, and identity carried by the one coming for help. Epston often refers to this kind of work as a sort of shared ethnography (an ethnographer collects and preserves the stories of a society and its members) where the consultant and consultee work together to best tell the care seeker's stories of value and meaning in a collaborative way. White talks about the counselor/consultant as one who is decentered (not carrying the defining expertise nor the expectation of outcome) but influential in the story development process. When the word *therapy* is used to describe this kind of work, the real novelty and benefit of cocreating narratives of identity, meaning, and value can get lost. Narrative pastoral care relies on this nonhierarchical, collaborative approach.

The word *narrative* may be even more problematic. This word usually serves as an equivalent for the word *story*, suggesting that both are about using language to tell or write *descriptively* about events or experiences. However, this notion of narrative as primarily descriptive doesn't fit with the way it is used in narrative therapy, where language is thought about in more creative and constructive ways, not just as a tool to be used to express and exchange ideas with others. Increasingly, the consensus among linguists has been built around the idea (and this is by no means a new idea) that language itself is constitutive. In other words, the way we develop and use language serves a creative function. Language creates the world we encounter through it even as we create language that describes that reality.[3]

When we invite people to "tell their story," as we often do in pastoral care, the story itself creates and reinforces their identity and meaning. So which story we invite people to tell matters. If we invite people only to talk about the stories that cause them pain or diminish who they are, then they are more likely to continue to experience that pain and those problematic identities as primary in their lives. The narrative practitioner always remembers that people are made up of a myriad of stories, not just problem stories. The goal of narrative therapy is sometimes characterized by the phrase "telling our stories in ways that make us stronger."[4] This phrase captures the notion that how people's stories are invited and how people are supported in remembering and telling those stories have real and lasting effects on their lives.

Narrative therapy is largely built around this assertion about the creative power of language as people tell their stories. The word *narrative*, then, as used in narrative therapy, has a very specific meaning that immediately translates into the way that caregivers invite stories from people who are seeking their help.

What Stories Do We Invite?

We as caregivers always listen to the stories of others through a particular lens or with a certain intention. There is no neutral or objective listening.[5] We are often unaware of the intention we have in asking a question or in the way we actively listen, but nonetheless, we invite people through a host of cues—through the questions we ask and the parts of the story we focus on—to tell their stories in particular ways. For example, suppose someone comes to my (Christie) office and says, "I am turning in my paper, but I had a hard time getting it done. I'm really struggling with time management. I feel like I'm not keeping up. I'm overwhelmed." I have several choices about how I respond. I could just say, "Thanks for dropping it off," where I politely indicate that I don't want to hear more of the story. I could say, "I'm sorry you are having trouble. What do you think is causing you to feel so overwhelmed?" which is often considered the most appropriate pastoral response. It focuses sympathetically on the problem with an eye toward finding the cause and, thus, hopefully a solution. Or I could ask, with honest curiosity, "Given how much work you've been faced with, how were you able to get this paper in on time?"

This last response invites the student to focus on aspects of their actions and identity that have allowed them to be successful and to which they haven't been paying much attention. And in the telling of that story of success, the reality of their successful experience becomes more tangible and available to them. The questions I ask, the intention I have in listening, shape the story to be told. This story, then, becomes a "narrative" of identity and meaning—a way used to think about, create, and experience the self.

We think it is useful to be clear about what kind of story we are inviting when we engage in pastoral care. Many counseling theories, especially those that are based on a medical or "scientific" model, urge us to invite the story of problems or "symptoms." The care seeker is asked to focus their attention on those aspects of their lives and identities that cause them problems or pain. Too often, those pains and problems have even become part of their identities ("I am depressed," "I am an addict," "I am codependent," for example). Narrative counselors are interested in all of the stories that are part of the care seeker's experience, not just the problem stories. So when a person using a narrative therapy approach listens to a care seeker, they listen very carefully to the struggles and heartaches that have brought them to seek help. The care companion serves as a compassionate presence to the care seeker amid the problems they are experiencing. They use all the listening skills that are available to them as they offer care and support. And as they are carefully listening, they work hard not to fall into the trap of identifying the care seeker with the problems they are describing. They keep the person's problems separate from the person's self-definition. (A narrative counseling mantra is "A person is a person, and a problem is a problem. A person is never a problem.") But a narrative-oriented caregiver, as they are supportively listening to the problem story, also is listening just as carefully for two other stories, neither of which may be initially spoken—(1) the "absent but implicit" story and (2) the "exceptional" story. These are the stories that have gone missing from the person's repertoire as the problem story (and identity) has gotten more dominant in their lives.

As we noted earlier, when problem stories begin to dominate a person's experience, the other stories of who they are and what they value often begin to get lost. For example, a person experiencing persistent sadness and insecurity may not be able to remember their former sense of self-confidence and anticipation. They forget that they are not only a person who feels sad and insecure much of the time but also a person who has hopes and plans that have guided their life. They may begin to feel that they are not even that hopeful person at all anymore. Yet as narrative therapy claims, "no problem story is 100 percent successful"[6] in erasing the other stories of identity and meaning that the person has valued. A preferred identity story is lurking underneath the more dominant problem story. There are at least two ways into those missing stories.

Absent but Implicit Stories

The "absent but implicit" story is exactly what it sounds like. The very story that the person tells suggests that there is another, contradictory story in the midst of it. For example, Stephen Madigan (a noted narrative therapy author and trainer) once talked about a couple who had come to him for therapy, telling him that they "bickered all the time." He perceived that clearly, they don't bicker all the time—that's not possible. So he asked them if it really was "all the time." When they said that it wasn't, he asked them what it was they did together when they weren't bickering. In this way, they were able to tell an "absent but implicit" story about other aspects of their relationship that they preferred over bickering but that they usually forgot about because the bickering had become their dominant narrative.[7] Another example comes from a workshop by David Epston, where he talked about a family who had come to him because the father, especially, was fed up with his teenage son. The father said that his son was a huge disappointment and unremitting failure. Looking for the absent but implicit story, Epston said to the father, "It sounds like you had a different idea of what a father and son relationship might be like. What was that idea?" The father was startled but began to talk about what he had wanted with his son—time together where they shared interests and ideas and took pleasure in the relationship. The son interrupted his father's telling, saying, "You've never told me that before. That's what I wanted too." Epston asked them whether they ever had even a glimpse of these things in their relationship. This led to the son and the father beginning to talk about a few times they remembered closeness together. This invited them, under the skilled guidance of Epston, to talk about what might be possible for them. The absent but implicit story was invited and made available for development, and this helped dislodge and disempower the unquestioned problematic identity story both the father and son had about their relationship.

Whenever a disappointment is expressed, it means there is also an implicit story of hope and possibility. Inviting this story into the room doesn't deny the problematic story, but it relativizes it. It makes room for there to be multiple ways to see the situation or the person's identity, and it allows new possibilities to emerge. As you can see, this approach to counseling is very different from one where the problem story sets all the rules for the conversation.

Exceptional Stories

The second story that narrative practitioners listen for is the "exceptional" story. This means that the story being invited and told is an exception to the problem story—it is the story of a situation or a time when the problem wasn't in charge of the person's identity, and they were able to experience a preferred sense of self. In the previous example, one can see both the implicit story ("Did you have an idea about what your father and son story might have looked like?") and the exceptional story ("Have there ever been times when you caught just a glimpse of that positive relationship?"). In the case of the exceptional story, a narrative-oriented consultant would listen to the story with an ear for when the story takes a turn that, as Michael White often said, the problem wouldn't predict. It suggests that there are exceptions to the problem story/identity when the person has a glimmer of the self they prefer. This glimmer is often quite fragile. The experiences that support it don't make it into the dominant narratives of the person's life. This exception to the problem story hasn't been given adequate significance by the person (or by the influential people or culture in their life), so it isn't able to stand in any contradictory way to the problem story.

For example, a young woman who came to talk to her pastor said that she had been in therapy for many years because of a history of childhood abuse. The therapy had been very helpful for her. She had received support, broken through the secrecy, and gotten to know other women who had similar experiences. Now, however, she felt that the primary way she thought about herself was as a survivor of abuse and as somewhat flawed by what she had survived. She said she knew that she had learned to maintain a barrier to keep herself safe and that this was part of her ongoing response to the abuse. She felt lonely, and when asked what she wished could be different, she said that she wished she had never experienced the abuse, because then she would have the option to be normal. (This perspective obviously leaves her stuck, since she can't undo this horrific reality.) But as she talked with the pastor, she mentioned that she had been with a group of women from the church over the weekend, and for a few hours, she had felt like her "real self" rather than this isolated, protected person she usually saw herself to be. The pastor, trained in narrative counseling ideas, immediately perceived this as an "exceptional moment" and, with a real sense of honest curiosity, began to discuss with the woman what that "real self" was like and how she had recognized her. As the conversation continued, the woman began to *be* her "real self" as she described what that felt like and also began to identify other times when she felt that she was experiencing her "real self" rather than the isolated self. Thus, the "real self" story became her reality as she told it (language being constructive, not just descriptive). After thirty minutes with the pastor, this woman had reshaped her hopes to the point of saying that what she wished could happen was that she could be her "real self" more often. She and the pastor were then able to explore what helped her recognize and live out that preferred identity and what tended to get in the way of her experiencing that "real self." When they had finished the conversation, the woman left her pastor's office with much greater access to the self she preferred to be and with a sense of what would help her stay in touch with that.

This story is a good example of the way that problem stories are never 100 percent successful in taking over a person's life—that other alternative and preferred stories coexist with the problem story. So the consultant has to stay alert to those potential stories. Two things have to happen in order to help exceptional moments (sometimes called "unique outcomes" or "sparkling moments") gain both voice and strength. First, the consultant has to notice the exception. This can be quite difficult because of its fleeting nature. Often, the unique outcome is offered as almost an aside in the telling and living of the more dominant problem story. So the consultant has to listen with an ear finely tuned for problem-story exceptions, really paying attention and taking notice when they appear. And second, when they hear the exception, the consultant has to become interested in it and curious about it, introducing that interest and curiosity into the conversation.

When I (Christie) teach about this idea to seminary students who are studying narrative therapy theory, I often use a metaphor from the Harry Potter books.[8] In those books, one of the favorite games of the young wizards and witches is Quidditch. The game, played in the air on broomsticks, is sort of a cross between basketball and field hockey with physical hazards tossed into the mix. It is a fast-paced game with the players all focused on the bludgers (the hazards that can be thrown at a player) and the quaffle (the ball that is to be thrown through the goal). But there is one player, the seeker, who doesn't participate in the fast-paced action but rather flies above the game, waiting and watching for the other ball—the tiny golden snitch. If that ball is captured during the game, the match ends, and the team that has captured the snitch gets three hundred points—enough points that they generally win. The small golden snitch is almost invisible as it flies quickly around with its tiny wings, but it is a prize worth waiting for. So when the seeker (the player looking for the snitch) sees it, they single-mindedly head for it, knowing that getting hold of this elusive but crucial part of the game is the biggest possible prize.

I think of unique outcomes (exceptional moments) as the golden snitch. While the consultant is certainly listening to and supporting the care seeker in all possible ways (i.e., valuing the action-packed game being played), their main task is not to get caught up in the problem story (the action on the field) but to watch for, pursue, and take hold of the unique outcome (the golden snitch). Doing so takes discipline, skill, persistence, and excellent boundaries, but it gives the care seeker the opportunity to lay claim to a lost or hidden identity story that will empower them in the face of the problems they are experiencing. Again, honest curiosity by the consultant drives the story development around this unique outcome.

Unique Outcome Development

As we've implied, it is not enough just to notice the absent but implicit story or the exceptional story. These stories need to be developed in the conversation between consultant and care seeker. The consultant's job is to ask honest and curious questions about this alternative story in such a way that it becomes full-bodied. In narrative therapy, this is called a "re-authoring conversation." When the story is richly told, it then has a chance to become strong enough to provide resources and identity for the care seeker in the midst of the problem story. It generates new perspectives, new experiences, and a way forward that better fits the person's hopes and values than the problem identity/story does. So the consultant asks what Stephen Madigan calls "beautiful questions."[9] These are questions that invite the care seeker to experience an alternative way of being, one they have known in other times or one that others know about them but that they have lost access to as the problem identity/story has gained dominance in their life. Not only does the consultant ask these beautiful questions, which we will explore in the next chapter, but they also ask story development questions, which help give this new story visibility and vitality. As the care seeker tells their story, they begin to recognize this "self" that has been inaccessible and to understand how important it is to who they are. The story begins to take some of the energy away from the problem identity and gives that energy to the reclaimed narrative as the care seeker gains agency in building a life that isn't ruled by the problem sense of self. The consultant might ask the care seeker about who in their life wouldn't be surprised by this exceptional story or who else knows these things about them. In this way, others who are important to the care seeker gain a voice in building this strong alternative story. The person literally re-members (re-connects with) the self they have been, and in telling those stories about who they have been, they become that person again.

Overview of a Narrative Therapy Process

In summary, the narrative therapy process flows in the following way. A narrative consultant works to help care seekers loosen the hold of the problem story on their lives so it doesn't serve to define them. Consultants usually do this by the way they reflectively listen to the problem story, referring to the person not as the problem but rather as being in relationship with the problem. The consultant would not talk about an angry person or a depressed person. They would talk about how anger (noun rather than adjective) tries to control the person's feelings and behavior, for example, or how sadness tries to keep the person at home instead of connecting with his or her friends.

This is called an "externalizing conversation" because it works against the person internalizing the problem as part of themselves and encourages them to see the problem as outside of who they are. In seeing the problem outside of themselves, they can get to know it and how it tries to take over the way they see themselves. In addition, they can look at cultural discourses and worldviews—like racism, sexism, or other value-laden belief systems—and how those have impacted or restricted their lives and their choices.

This work of externalizing and deconstructing makes room for other exceptional or unique stories to surface, stories about times when the problem wasn't in charge or where the person has an experience that the problem story wouldn't predict. These are the unique moments that are windows into identities and values that the person prefers to live out. These exceptional moments that surface in the storytelling are often fragile and underdeveloped. They've been shrouded by the problem story much of the time, so they require careful attention and story development. The narrative consultant asks a variety of questions that develop the alternative story in rich and compelling ways. It makes the identity that resides in that story much more accessible to the person. This is a re-authoring conversation and is at the heart of the consultative process.

Not only is the exceptional moment richly developed in the re-authoring conversation, but together, the consultant and care seeker also locate that preferred identity in other experiences that have occurred over time. In addition, the re-authored story is further strengthened through re-membering conversations where the care seeker is invited to recall other people who have generated and supported these preferred identities at various times in their life. As the alternative story becomes more readily available to the care seeker, they are able to live their identity, values, and agency more in keeping with it. And the alternative story continues to deconstruct the power and significance of the problem story and identity.

As you can tell from reading our summary of narrative therapy, this approach meets the criteria we set out at the beginning of the chapter. First, it pays attention to the context and culture from which problem stories are often born and through which they are maintained. All our experiences are seen in light of the cultural discourses in which we live. Second, narrative therapy puts the life experiences and values of the care seeker at the heart of the consultation and decenters both the so-called expert knowledge of the consultant and the fixed social descriptions of health and normalcy. It makes room for diverse experiences and values and trusts the care seeker to define those with integrity. Third, the approach invites transparency between the consultant and the care seeker and generates a consultative and collaborative relationship.

And fourth, it is a value-based approach, grounded not in medical models of health and pathology but rather in a philosophy of empowerment, justice, and community.

We find that a narrative-based approach is well suited for congregational care. In the past, our focus and that of the majority of programs for training congregational members to do pastoral care has been on active listening, which is, of course, a continuing key component of all good caregiving. Yet this singular focus risks giving encouragement and support to problem stories, strengthening those at the cost of potential stories that "make people stronger." When the problem story is more richly described in the pastoral conversation than any alternative and resource-filled narrative, then increased pain and suffering may be unintentionally caused.

Alternatively, when training programs focus on a more problem-solving, advice-giving, and goal-oriented approach, as some do, there is a significant risk that the caregiver's perspective, instead of the care seeker's, becomes the focal point of the care relationship. The caregiver uses their own identity, expertise, and value system to shape the care seeker's journey, thereby imposing direction and solutions that usually have minimal relevance for the care seeker's own particular life. In addition, when the caregiver offers or imposes specific advice or problem-solving direction, it tends to diminish both the care seeker's agency and confidence, and the problem story continues to be in charge of the person's identity and focus. A narrative orientation to pastoral care avoids both of these problem approaches (symptom focused or overly directive) and instead promotes a collaborative relationship that offers support for problem stories while inviting empowering alternative stories.

Ideas to Carry Forward

We would hope that the reader carries a few central ideas from this discussion of narrative therapy theory into the rest of the book. First, deconstruction—the task of helping people separate themselves from both the cultural truth claims that have supported the problem stories of their lives and the problem identity itself—is essential in making room for an alternative story to emerge. As we said earlier, people are people, not problems, and when a problem has served to define a person's life, much of the richness of that life is made invisible and unavailable. Helping the person separate from the problem story makes space for the person to find the other stories of their life that make a richer and more authentic identity possible.

Second, in a narrative approach, care companions pay attention to the hidden stories in care seekers' lives that hold the promise of preferred identity, agency, and meaning. These are the elements of a person's life that have not been valued or supported or that have been lost to the burden of the problems in their life. These hints or clues of preferred stories are known by various names in narrative therapy theory—sparkling moments, unique outcomes, exceptions to the problem story—and they are always present in the person's life as they talk about the problem-saturated story they are experiencing. A narrative consultant's intention is to stay alert to and interested in these windows into the care seeker's more empowering narrative.

Third, we would suggest that care companions ask themselves what story they want to invite when listening to a care seeker. Of course, lay care companions are attentive to and supportive of all the struggles and difficulties that brought the person into a care relationship. Yet once the clues (exceptional moments) to the person's preferred narrative surface in the conversation, the care companion may be able to invite the person to develop those empowering possibilities. As we have said, this re-authoring process is key to a narrative approach. This story development process is not to replace the problem story but rather to disempower the problem story's primacy.

Finally, the fourth idea to carry from this chapter is that the care companion and care seeker are collaborators who, together, in the midst of the problem story, coinvestigate the hints of preferred stories and coauthor those stories into lived experience. The process is a shared enterprise and includes deep respect, careful listening, a commitment to the local wisdom of the care seeker, and a belief in the strength, resiliency, and complexity of people's lives.

These ideas about pastoral care, drawn from narrative therapy theory, are not just for caregiving work. Believing that people aren't defined by their problem stories and that there is always so much more to a person than the problems they are struggling with can be a very fruitful way for us to see one another day to day. Just as care companions need to be aware of the intention and perspective they bring to their pastoral listening, all of us need to be intentional about how we regard one another. We can bring this commitment to inviting the stories "that make us stronger" to all our interactions in the church.

In the next chapter, we will explore four key practices of narrative pastoral care and their implications both for pastoral conversation and for teaching this method to lay care companions. Those four practices are narrative attitude, narrative presence, narrative listening, and narrative questioning. Of course, this approach to lay pastoral care contains more than just the development of these practices. Other key issues such as maintaining boundaries and practicing confidentiality, exploring the use of spiritual and religious resources, and studying the dynamics of various pastoral situations (like grieving, illness, and so on) are also important. Yet we want to start with these four practices because they most clearly reflect the philosophy of our narrative approach.

A QUESTION TO CONSIDER: How does narrative therapy theory understand the nature of storytelling in a care relationship, especially as it invites the story that "makes us stronger"?

3

Narrative Practices for Lay Pastoral Care

As we move into some of the practices that inform both the subject matter for lay pastoral caregiving and our proposed teaching methods, it is important to remember that the purpose of this book is to help prepare people in congregations to engage in pastoral care with people who are seeking that kind of relationship, usually because of a crisis, a major transition, or some other challenging situation in their lives. Our vision is that this preparation for pastoral conversation isn't limited to just a few people who volunteer to be part of a ministry team. Our hope is that, over time, many people in the congregation will be trained to engage in pastoral conversation at some level. We believe that the more people who are trained to engage in meaningful pastoral care with folks experiencing hardships or crises, the healthier and more engaged the congregation as a whole will be. A congregation with a significant number of trained care companions will more naturally be alert to the needs of their fellow congregants, be better able to respond appropriately to those needs, and be more engaged in the congregation as a whole.

The needs and training for lay pastoral caregiving can vary. When a congregant is experiencing an intensive crisis like a bereavement, a health problem, or a major life change, a care companion with more extensive training is most helpful. We sometimes call people who minister to others in more acute crises or transitions "pastoral companions." They commit to engaging in a pastoral care relationship with a care seeker over a limited amount of time, usually up to a year, to companion them through a challenging, life-changing event. Pastoral care for these life transitions calls for a more intensive training program that includes significant exposure to narrative listening and questioning as well as appropriate subject material relevant to those crises.

Other care teams might have less extensive training, depending on the situations in which they offer pastoral care. For example, teams that are primarily oriented to care for chronic situations of pastoral need—isolation, loneliness, disappointments, and so forth—will benefit from training that focuses on ethics and boundaries as well as pastoral attitudes, presence, and listening but not the more intensive training of narrative theory or the subject matter related to crisis-oriented care. They may offer connection and conversation—perhaps for the long term—by phone, handwritten notes, face-to-face conversations, and/or internet visits.

Other potential care teams might be more spontaneous—"pop-up" care—where the members offer pastoral care in immediate, short-term situations, such as a few days after a person returns home from hospitalization or welcomes a new addition to the family. Or as in a recent situation, a team of care companions may be organized to reach out to congregational members for connection and conversation by phone, note, or internet when they are all isolated by the restrictions of a pandemic. The training for these kinds of groups would of course still include issues of ethics, boundaries, and presence but might also incorporate specific preparation for the concerns they are addressing (e.g., phone visitation for the pandemic lockdown or very short-term connections for those with a new baby).

The point here is that individual congregational members will have different gifts, interests, and callings that make them better suited to one kind of pastoral care ministry over another. Assessing an individual's fit and inviting them to consider various types of ministry is part of developing a congregation-wide network of pastoral care that supports the diverse needs of congregants and empowers a significant portion of the congregation to provide care.

Whatever kinds of care teams a congregation chooses to develop, having people trained in disciplined pastoral conversation to companion those in need will make a difference to the well-being of the whole church. Jeanne Stevenson-Moessner, a professor of pastoral care, in her important book *A Primer in Pastoral Care*, shares a minister's case study about her congregation. She writes that Arley, the sole pastor of a small congregation, takes a fall and ends up with serious neck and spine injuries. These injuries mean that he has to step away from his pastorate, and by doing that, he will lose his salary and his home. However, his wife, Peggy (the subject of the case study), tells the congregation that she will move into the role of full-time lay minister as long as three conditions are met. First, someone would drive her husband to physical therapy three times a week. Second, the congregation would find a way to provide childcare for her family. And third, the congregants would pick up the work of pastoral visitation/care. The church agrees to meet these conditions. Peggy writes, "As

Arley reached a milestone in recovery, so did the church. They seemed to come alive, with a renewed sense of hope, because they had been empowered to do ministry themselves. They began to regain some of the spirit of community they had lost and started to reach out to one another."[1] Empowering the congregation to engage in pastoral ministry with one another can often bring a church new life.

The Nature of Pastoral Conversation

One of the most important training elements for lay caregiving is helping the participants learn how to offer support and encouragement to someone experiencing hardship. Doug Purnell, an Australian pastoral theologian, gives a glimpse into the nature of such support when he writes, "When carers are present to others . . . without trying to change them . . . they are engaging in pastoral conversation. . . . Conversation is pastoral when there is a desire to care, when people attend to and listen to the other with discipline, and when that listening is about the living of the other."[2] Purnell raises key points that help us see that we are talking about not just a casual friendly connection but rather a thoughtful activity of ministry. First, pastoral conversation comes out of compassion and engagement. Without real care for the other, listening can become mechanical and detached. Anyone can learn how to engage in the techniques of careful listening, but if there is no real desire to care for the other, then this effort falls short of ministry. Yet there is a paradox in this. If all one brings to the conversation is emotional connection, especially if that connection is based on sympathy (processing another person's experience primarily through its connection to one's own experience), then the care companion may begin inadvertently to claim the experiences of the care seeker as their own—as if the situation or problem is theirs rather than belonging to the care seeker.

A second point Purnell makes is that pastoral conversation requires listening with discipline. Pastoral care companions need to be thoughtful and careful in the way they engage in pastoral conversation. Although pastoral care is largely about a committed ministry of presence, it's also about the disciplined use of certain skills, including the arts of pastoral conversation. Listening with discipline involves careful monitoring of boundaries and thoughtful awareness of the context in which the conversation is taking place as well as attention to one's own thoughts and feelings in response to the conversation. Pastoral conversation, as Purnell suggests, is not about "going with your gut" but rather about empathic attentiveness focused on inviting the care seeker's story and tending to that story with disciplined skills.

And Purnell makes the third point when he says that the "listening is about the living of the other." Only the care seeker has the storytelling rights (a common narrative description) to their own experience. Pastoral conversation is not about the care companion finding points in common with the care seeker, as if it is their shared story. This work is about inviting, receiving, and witnessing the storytelling of the other. It is about empathy (trying to hear and see the experience of the care seeker through the other's perspective rather than through one's own), not sympathy. Two friends might share the back-and-forthness of shared experiences, but pastoral care ensures that the conversation is primarily about the living of the other in all its complexities and contradictions. When the storytelling rights remain the purview of the care seeker, then the care companion is free to feel deep compassion, care, and even curiosity while at the same time letting go of the need or the right to invest in the outcome or direction of the care seeker's story. We could call this stance one of compassionate detachment. The storytelling, including the directions the story will take, belongs to the care seeker. The care companion lets go of directing or even expecting a particular outcome, even while they feel deep connection and compassion for the care seeker.

This larger notion of pastoral conversation is grounded in and facilitated by the four practices we named at the end of chapter 2. We begin with the notion of narrative attitude, since it serves as the foundation for the other practices. Narrative attitude communicates the philosophical commitments of narrative theory, setting the context for the other three practices.

Narrative Attitude

The most fundamental aspect of lay caregiving is the pastoral attitude—a combination of compassion, respect, trust, and commitment—that the care companion brings to it. Often, when we begin teaching communication skills to pastoral care students, their focus moves to the skills themselves, the technical side of pastoral communication. This can put their pastoral attitude in jeopardy, at least temporarily. We are convinced that the techniques of pastoral care communication can be taught and learned, but it is much harder to learn how to live and minister within a pastoral care attitude.

When we talk about a narrative attitude, we are suggesting that it is prior to and necessary for the other practices of presence, listening, and questioning. This understanding of narrative attitude is made up of several elements.

One of these elements is a sense of optimism that whatever the problem is in another person's life, they are not defined by it. People are always complex and multistoried, and no problem, no matter what it is, is completely successful in taking over a person's life. There is always more to a person than the pain or trouble they are experiencing. This conviction needs to be an important part of a care companion's approach to pastoral care. It is what helps them listen not only to the problem story being told but to all the other stories, implied or exceptional, that also make up the life and potential of the care seeker. To provide empowering and hopeful care, the care companion needs to commit themselves to the belief that the care seeker is made up of a myriad of experiences and gifts, even as they themselves may have lost sight of all but the problem story that seems to define them.

This belief that the care seeker is always more than the problem story in their life is related to several other dimensions of a narrative attitude. One of those is that the care seeker has full storytelling rights in the care relationship. The care seeker's story is always front and center. This may seem self-evident, since it is the care seeker's story that brings us to the relationship in the first place. Yet the care seeker's story can become displaced by the care companion if this attitude isn't a core commitment. It is all too common that care companions take ownership of the care seeker's story through a variety of means. Sometimes care companions become overinvolved in the story, letting their own feelings and anxieties get triggered, as if the story belonged somehow to them or they were experiencing it along with the care seeker. Sometimes care companions take over the story by beginning to feel or act as if the difficulties conveyed by the story are theirs to solve or fix. They bring their experience to bear on the story, providing "solutions" for the care seeker to try on. These attempts to solve or fix or advise generally come out of the care companion's experience of anxiety. This may emerge when hearing the care seeker's story but sometimes arises when the care seeker requests advice or a solution. Even in those cases, however, the care companion must remember whose story this is, whose meaning and identity are at stake, and whose ongoing narrative is being constructed.

The care companion invites the storytelling; listens carefully to all the stories, including those not yet spoken; and encourages the care seeker to find the stories that bring them meaning and that ultimately make them stronger. But the care companion stays decentered in that process. It is not the care companion's meaning or identity that is center stage but the care seeker's. Although the care seeker and the care companion engage collaboratively in the telling and receiving and meaning-making of the story, the care seeker is the one who makes sense of the story being told and chooses the direction in which it will continue to move. The care companion is, of course, influential through the kinds of responses they offer, the questions they ask, and the way they encourage and receive the story. They must be careful and transparent in the way they mediate that influence. But the collaboration is defined by the care seeker, who is the storyteller and meaning-maker. The care companion is the receiver and witness to the story being told.

As people are invited to share their stories in empowering ways, they may also begin to shift their own narratives of meaning and identity. That shift has real effects on their lives. When we, as care companions, bring attitudes of decentering ourselves so that the full storytelling rights belong to and are expressed by the care seeker, we are doing so because of a deep belief that language constructs realities and re-authoring narratives changes lives. Let us give an example.

Margaret was telling her parish companion that she was feeling helpless and hopeless in light of her new cancer diagnosis. She was used to being strong and independent, and she didn't have any idea how to face this "sign of my weakness." "Maybe I shouldn't bother with treatment. Maybe it's just my time, even though the doctors are saying that there are good protocols for this kind of cancer." At this point, Margaret described herself as helpless and reported spending a lot of time just sitting and feeling hopeless, behaviors that were unlike her before her diagnosis.

Her lay companion asked her to talk a bit more about what she meant when she said she was used to being strong, and Margaret told stories about how she frequently helped people who were in crisis and needed support. She was the one on whom people called for help. As she told those stories, her voice became stronger, and she sat up straighter. The lay companion then asked her if she had ever used those skills and attitudes on her own behalf. She answered quickly, "Oh, yes, I have solved many problems in my own life through grit and determination."

When asked to tell a story about such an experience, she talked about a time when she was trying to figure out how to pay the bills and get an education at the same time. She almost gave up on college but was able to figure out how to alternate a semester of school with a semester of work while also caring for her elderly grandmother. The companion asked her, "Was that a time of strength or weakness or something else?" After thinking for a moment, she looked at the care companion and said, with some surprise, "It was both strength and weakness, and I think I am in a similar kind of moment in my life now."

When asked to say some more about that, Margaret went on to describe how this illness had made her feel weak, but in talking about who she had been all her life, she realized that she was also the same strong person—that the weakness hadn't replaced the strength, but it was calling out for her to use her strength and "grit." After a bit more conversation and with tears in her eyes, Margaret said, "I remember who I am now. Thank you for helping remind me." When Margaret left the room, she walked out with her head up, her back straight, and a sense of purpose on her face. She had become who she re-membered herself to be, and that helped move her experience of cancer forward in a new way.

In this situation, the care companion brought an attitude of respect and compassion and also an appreciation for the many layers of identity—including one of helplessness, one of grit and strength, and so on—that Margaret had, even in the midst of a major crisis. The care companion listened carefully to the crisis story and also listened to other stories that Margaret alluded to but hadn't reclaimed during this cancer crisis.

Helping people reclaim narratives that have been lost or forgotten can change their lives by giving them a chance to find meaning and identity that may have become unavailable or inaccessible during the current crisis. A lay companion with a narrative attitude remembers that language has powerful potential, that life narratives shape a person's identity and thus can enable them to take actions in ways that are life-giving, and that companioning work includes inviting empowering stories that may have been subsumed by the problems in care seekers' lives. A narrative attitude respects and supports people in the struggles they are experiencing while at the same time helping the care companion see the bigger picture—the absent but implicit stories and the exceptional stories that may have become invisible in the face of the problems. This commitment to "double listening"—listening to both the problems and related feelings as well as the absent but implicit stories of possibility—is core to a narrative attitude. We will explore this more fully when we discuss narrative listening and questioning.

Narrative Presence

Pastoral presence has been understood for many decades to be a key element of pastoral care. Modern pastoral care, from the 1950s on, was largely influenced by the theories of humanist psychologist Carl Rogers, who coined the term *unconditional positive regard* as a description of the importance of being fully present to and supportive of the care seeker. Mainline modern pastoral care followed that model to a large extent and encouraged students to develop ways of conveying their attentiveness and encouragement to the care seeker. Respect for the care seeker's own personhood and autonomy became central to good pastoral care.

Pastoral presence is the way a care companion communicates to a care seeker their deep respect, their focus on being a companion to the care seeker during hard times, and their compassionate attentiveness to the experience of the care seeker. It conveys the care companion's attentiveness to the well-being of the care seeker and a promise to do no harm in that pastoral relationship. But in addition to communicating the pastoral commitments of the care companion, pastoral presence also symbolically suggests the care of the congregation for the care seeker and, at some level, even the care of God. A care companion cannot just go through the motions of visiting a care seeker. They must genuinely desire the well-being of that person. A ministry of presence is ultimately about the authenticity of the care companion in their relationship with the care seeker.

When we talk about a narrative pastoral presence, we are talking about the care companion acting in a way that communicates all the commitments we named in the discussion on narrative attitude. So it is not just about wanting the best for the care seeker and engaging in attentive, compassionate presence. It is also about communicating the care companion's commitment to the care seeker's storytelling rights and the boundaries that are part of that. A narrative presence conveys the collaborative nature of pastoral care. The care companion consistently invites the care seeker to share their experience in all its complexity, attends to the struggles the care seeker is experiencing, and remembers that the care seeker is much more than the struggles. Through a narrative presence, a care companion always seeks to both support and empower the other. The companion listens to the wholeness of the other while inviting them to find their own wholeness in the storytelling. They convey a trust in the other—a trust in their wisdom and strength even in the midst of their pain. Narrative presence provides a safe and hospitable environment for the pastoral conversation and the pastoral relationship.

NARRATIVE LISTENING

As we explored in chapter 2, the work of listening in a narrative approach to care is not just about the strategies that allow the care companion to fully receive and witness the experience of the care seeker. It also focuses on the question of what we are listening for. In narrative listening, we work to tune in fully to the storytelling of the other (single listening), and we also listen to what is hinted at but not yet said (double listening). This combination of single and double listening is what is unique to a narrative approach, and both are central to this project.

THE NATURE OF SINGLE LISTENING

Nothing is more central to the ministry of pastoral care than careful, respectful, compassionate listening. It is the vehicle for trust building and connection. It is a way for the care seeker to open themselves up to share their concerns and struggles and for the care companion to receive those and bear witness to them. Single listening, or the act of listening to what is overtly being said, is more familiarly known as active listening. Disciplined active listening demonstrates to the care seeker the care companion's commitment to them and to the experience of support and healing in which they are engaged.

What is it that we mean when we talk about active listening? Since we communicate all the time with one another, the temptation is to believe that we already know what good listening looks like and that we are able to do it. But active listening as we are defining it here is a very specific approach to engaging in conversation. In active listening, the goal is threefold. First, we use active listening to convey to the care seeker that their story matters and that we are there for them. When we focus our attention fully on the care seeker's experience, we convey to them that we are ready to receive them for who they are and that we are committed to the care relationship.

Second, through active listening, we attempt to hear the other person at the various levels in which they communicate—

including content, context, tone, and body and facial expressions—so that we are able to enter empathically into the world of the care seeker. It is important to listen to all of these dimensions without drawing fixed notions of what they mean or how they should be interpreted. It is also important that we take in these levels of communication without contaminating them with our own biases and assumptions. We listen with discipline and focus to all of these dimensions of communication.

The third goal of active listening is to let the other person know that they have been accurately heard. When a person has been heard and understood, then they are free to continue the story with confidence that the listener is following along and taking it in. In the process, they may even hear themselves differently or with new insights. When a care seeker does not feel understood or heard, then they tend to either repeat themselves so that the listener will be able to understand them, or depending on how they interpret the lack of understanding, they may stop trying to share the nature of their experience altogether. The way to let the other person know they have been accurately heard is to reflect back to them, tentatively, in the listener's own words or through paraphrasing, what they think they have heard. The focus is on the content, informed by the act of "listening" to all of the other dimensions named previously (feelings, body language, context, and tone). The listener's response should be tentative, with an uplifted or questioning tone at the end, so that the speaker can easily correct something that has been misunderstood or that is incomplete. The listener's next response acknowledges and incorporates the correction so that the speaker knows they have been understood or can offer another correction.

The art of reflecting the speaker's story back to them so that it can be confirmed is a challenging one. While the concept is straightforward, the ability to smoothly respond to a speaker with a reflective response that doesn't interrupt them, interpret them, or truncate their meaning is one that can never be perfectly achieved. Those of us who wish to be effective listeners need to learn the skills and practices of active listening, as well as those behaviors that get in their way, by consistent and persistent practice. Listening with the kind of intentionality and effectiveness that it requires to move into another's world, and into the particular crisis or need of the care seeker, is difficult and involves a disciplined commitment to the person being listened to. If you have ever been listened to with this kind of commitment to your well-being, you understand the importance of this kind of care. It is a rare and precious gift. The speaker's response to effective active listening is generally an affirmation of some sort, like a "yes" or a "that's right," and then moving on with the story. It becomes part of a natural and flowing conversation.

Blocks to Active Listening

As pastoral theologian Emma Justes said in her book *Hearing beyond the Words*, "The problem with listening is that it is so easy not to do."[3] There are many things that get in the way of effective listening. One of those blocks comes from the habits we have for everyday conversation, such as our rather natural desire to make sense of what we hear by comparing it to our own experience. This usually means that we end up focusing on our experience or our interpretations of our experience and assuming it is similar to that being told to us by the care seeker. We begin to make assumptions about what the person is feeling or the direction in which they should take the story. As we said earlier, sometimes we want to actively join the care seeker's story by falling into the "me too" habit of conversation where we share a similar (or assumed similar) experience. This moves the focus from the care seeker's story to the care companion's. These kinds of "shared experience" habits are generally not appropriate in a time of active listening. When engaged in the process of active listening, any self-disclosure should only occur when it is clearly in the service of inviting the care seeker's story.

Four other dynamics may get in the way of active listening. The first is our desire to put the care seeker's experiences or feelings in our familiar categories as a way to understand them or manage our feelings about them. For example, if a person tells me about her sadness, her quietness, and her withdrawnness, I might begin to think in the category of depression. Or I might decide that this person is really similar to a classmate I once had or a relative of mine. Once we begin to think of a person's experiences through a certain category, we usually listen and pay attention to only the things that fit with that categorization. If I'm thinking of depression, then I don't listen for the feelings and experiences the care seeker is talking about that contradict that depression story. We tend to find what we look for. In this way, the care seeker's story gets distorted, and we try to guide the story in the direction that fits our assumptions about it.

A second dynamic is our tendency to want to lead the story in a particular direction. It might be the kind of leading discussed earlier where we want to continue to confirm our assumptions or categories for the story. Or it might be leading the story in ways that make us feel better—maybe trying to cheer the person up or contradict what we think is a painful story. Or it might be that we want to lead the person in a direction that nudges them toward a solution we would like to see them embrace. All of these (or any other) habits of trying to direct a person's story in ways that fit our desires for them are generally problematic. It means that we are, overtly or subtly, trying to take away the storytelling rights of the care seeker.

The most common reason for story-leading is the almost universal desire on the part of lay care companions (and care companions in general) to advise the care seeker or fix their pain or, in some form or another, offer solutions and directions that will "make the person feel better." This tendency to want to advise or fix is ubiquitous. It slips into our responses without our even recognizing it. Sometimes we form it as a question (e.g., "Have you tried . . . ?" or "Wouldn't you like to . . . ?"). Sometimes it is just straightforward advice (e.g., "If I were you, I would . . ." or "I think you would feel better if you . . ."). This desire to fix the other is often more of a desire to fix ourselves, to feel less anxious or less distressed about the pain of the other. It also can come out of an honest desire to make the care seeker feel better. Yet this advising and fixing and trying to make the care seeker feel better do not belong to the role of the lay care companion. As we have said, the role of the lay care companion is to actively listen, to support and witness the experience of the care seeker, to witness the care seeker's journey, and ultimately, to help them tell the story in ways that will be empowering to them.

A third dynamic that may get in the way of effective active listening results from the various kinds of biases we all carry and that impact the way we relate to the people we encounter. For example, I may be affected by someone's gender, race, class, sexual orientation, employment, age, appearance, speech pattern, and so on. Someone may remind me of my second cousin who had the same problem or the same hair color. Or a care seeker might be dealing with a problem similar to one that I have had, and I might be biased as to how they should think about that problem. All of these and other biases may move us toward a greater appreciation of a person or toward a negative evaluation of a person, or we may be fairly neutral in how it impacts our view. Yet bias keeps us from seeing the person in front of us as someone with their own unique experience. Although we all have biases of all kinds, the key is to be aware of them so that when they occur, we are able to recognize them for what they are and put them aside so that the care seeker's story and experience can be seen for what it is.

The fourth dynamic to be named (although this list is by no means exhaustive) has to do with the risks of focusing on our own performance. When we become self-conscious about how we are doing in a pastoral care visit and whether we are being helpful to the care seeker, we tend to lose our ability to be fully present and engaged with them. We begin to lose the focus that this visit is about receiving the care seeker's story and, instead, focus on whether we are good enough in our facilitating of it. It is, at the very least, a distraction from our pastoral presence. Similarly, other kinds of distractions may get in the way. Those might include whatever feelings or worries that we are having in our lives that unintentionally get carried into the visit. Again, the key is to notice these distractions, whether they are performance worries or other kinds of life concerns that we are carrying, and to intentionally put them aside so we can focus on the care seeker and the pastoral conversation in which we are engaged. The more we practice this, like all of the other skills of active listening and pastoral conversation, the better we will get at being able to invite and support the care seeker's story.

Not all conversation with a care seeker needs to be facilitated through active listening. Certainly, at the beginning of a visit, there is often the kind of back-and-forth sharing that helps build rapport and connection. And there are often times during a visit when a care seeker prefers to be in casual conversation rather than what might be called purpose-filled conversation. However, the care companion needs to be attentive to cues that signal the sharing of a meaningful experience or feeling by the care seeker so that they can quickly shift into active listening in response to that cue. Active listening should always be the default position for the care companion. It lets the care seeker know that the visit is focused on their needs and experiences, not the care companion's.

STRATEGIES FOR ACTIVE LISTENING

Assuming that we are able to recognize these roadblocks to active listening, the question remains: How do we avoid them? First, we continue to stay conscious of our commitments to both a narrative attitude and a narrative presence. We try to convey those in the way we engage in this pastoral relationship. It is helpful to prepare for the conversation by reminding ourselves of what beliefs and commitments we are bringing into this relationship and to remain centered so we are able to mediate an authentic pastoral presence. That said, we have to remember that we listen with our whole selves to the whole self of the other. That means we are comfortable, we are in a place that minimizes distractions and offers privacy, and we have attentive behaviors like appropriate eye contact, open body and facial language, and an appropriate space between us. Gerard Egan uses the mnemonic device of SOLER[4] to help remember some of the behaviors that convey both attentiveness and hospitality. The words associated with this acronym are used in these guidelines:

- Face the care receiver *squarely*.
- Adopt an *open* body posture.
- *Lean* slightly forward.
- Maintain *eye* contact.
- Stay *relaxed*.

These behaviors are not absolute. For example, for some people, direct eye contact would be uncomfortable or would convey a more confrontational approach rather than a welcoming message. This could be a cultural issue or a personal one. Sitting squarely across from someone might be very helpful and inviting for one person but feel too challenging for another. Chairs set at more of an angle where both conversation partners can easily see each other's faces might be a much more comfortable arrangement. The point is that to convey our commitment to the care seeker and to the conversation, we must be intentional in the way we relate to the person we are visiting. This is the beginning of the listening process.

Active listening requires intentionality, focus, and persistent practice. Learning and practicing the skills and attitudes of active listening should be part of virtually every training session of the lay pastoral care groups.

As we said, active listening might be characterized as "single" listening. We are listening to the story being told: clarifying it, receiving it, inviting it forward, and serving as a witness to it. We listen to the words, and we "listen" to the body language, facial expressions, tone of voice, and contexts in which it is taking place. It is single listening because we are taking in the story as it is—receiving it as the care seeker offers it. This is key to the pastoral care process and should be the default position of the care companion. However, sometimes single listening has limitations, especially if it reinforces and perpetuates a story that is damaging to the care seeker's preferred sense of self. In these cases, it is important to begin a process of "double listening."

Double Listening

Narrative listening clearly builds on the base of active listening but is especially characterized by "double listening" because we not only listen to and reflect the story that is being told but also listen to stories that exist in the gaps. As we noted earlier, these are the absent but implicit stories and the exceptional stories.

These stories exist as resources for the storyteller but haven't been given enough significance to allow them to compete with the problem story's dominance in defining the storyteller. They are reflections of the care seeker's experience, but they have become inaccessible to them. For example, a story of disappointment implies that the person hoped for or expected a different outcome. Sometimes that different outcome holds an ongoing vision for them. Or a tiny "aside" in a story may hold an "exception" that challenges the "rule" of the problem story. Narrative listening fully receives the story that the care seeker wishes to tell, knowing that this is not the only story that defines them.

The benefit and the limitation of active (single) listening is that by deeply listening to the story, the care companion validates and encourages it. This works well and can be powerfully supportive and affirming in most cases, especially when the story is one that needs to be told for the well-being of the speaker. The story, in this case, helps the care seeker feel stronger and more integrated. However, narrative listening (double listening) is needed when the story being told is a disempowering one for the care seeker and which, through its telling, begins to take on a more negative life-defining power as it is told and retold.

Active listening always needs to be the starting point and primary focus in lay care ministry. However, the care companion needs to be attentive to the stories not yet spoken, implicit or exceptional, when they see that the problem story is feeding pain, injustice, or a diminished sense of self. In other words, the care companion does not want to enrich a story that is doing harm to the care seeker. We have to be careful how we invite people to tell their stories so that we don't make their suffering more vivid or defining. This doesn't mean we try to talk the care seeker out of their story or distract them with "feel good" messages or give "helpful" advice. It does mean that we listen with one ear to the story being told, but we also listen to the stories that are implied or hinted at that might provide a slight shift for the storyteller—a shift that calls into question the defining nature of the problem story they are telling about themselves.

For example, a care seeker tells his care companion that he has always been a bad student in school ("I guess I'm just pretty stupid"). But as he continues to describe his school experience, he mentions a teacher in a creative writing class who saw something more in him. This was said in a casual way, as an "aside." But the care companion notices this "exception" and says, "Could I just ask you something about that teacher?" After receiving permission, the care companion asks, "What do you think this teacher saw in you that other teachers missed?" The care seeker began to talk about the poetry and stories he wrote back then and that he had thought about becoming a writer. As this story is invited and supported, a lost self-image begins to reemerge, one that gives the care seeker a new sense of self and vision.

Strategies for Double Listening

There are two primary ways to engage in active narrative listening. The first way is one of the most familiar features of a narrative approach and is called "externalized listening."[5] In this activity, as the listener carefully hears the problematic story, they use language that separates the person from the problem in their active listening. It assumes that a person isn't defined by a problem but rather is in relationship with a problem that is trying to define them. If a person says that they have been hopeless this past week, the listener reflects something like, "So hopelessness has been a constant companion to you this past week." The simple shift from the word *hopeless*, an adjective that defines the person (i.e., "I am hopeless"), to *hopelessness*, a noun that is distinct from the person (i.e., "hopelessness has become your companion"), gives a sense of distance between the problem (hopelessness) and the person who is much more than the hopelessness they are experiencing. Or suppose the care companion is listening attentively to a problem-filled story with care and compassion, never rushing to change it, and while telling that story, the care seeker says, "I am an anxious person. I worry all of the time. I feel scared and alone." The care companion, in reflecting that, says, "So anxiety is all around you, and when it closes in on you,

you feel worried and frightened and alone. Is that right?" This subverts the internalizing process where the care seeker identifies with the problem. This distance can allow them to see themselves more holistically and to look at the problem, which has seemed overwhelming and absolute, in a more relativized way. The listener doesn't need to do any more than use this linguistic shift in their reflections, but it can make a big difference in allowing room for other, more empowering stories to surface in the ongoing story. The storyteller often will respond with a statement like, "That's an interesting way to say that. I've never thought of it that way before." The key to externalizing listening is to be consistent with using the noun in reflecting the story to the person rather than switching back and forth between adjective and noun.

A second way to do narrative listening is for the care companion to reflect to the care seeker, in their active listening, an acknowledgment of the absent but implicit story[6] that has been hinted at in the storytelling but not articulated. For example, a care seeker is describing to her care companion how she has no energy, motivation, or interest in being with other people. She says that she used to love entertaining but just doesn't feel like she can do it anymore. A little later in the conversation, when the care seeker is bringing a cup of coffee to the care companion, she apologizes for the house not being as neat as she would like it to be because she had some people over the day before. The care companion, aware of the contradiction between this statement and earlier statements about the lack of energy and interest to be with others, responds, "So you had a gathering here this weekend." By giving this basic reflective response, she invites an alternative story to the earlier story. The care seeker responds, "I did. My grandson turned eight, and his mother had no interest in having his friends over for a party, so I said that I would do it. I had ten little eight-year-olds here, and my, what a lot of energy they had. They are so cute at that age." The care companion responds, "What was it like to offer that gift of a party to your grandson?" The care seeker says, with enthusiasm in her voice, "It made me so happy to see him happy. I loved being able to make him a birthday cake. I had gone out to buy some party favors, and the kids all thought they were great." The care companion continues to invite details of this story of energy and engagement through active listening and finally asks, "Did it surprise you that you were able to push away your low energy to provide such a great experience for your grandson?" The care seeker responds, "You know, now that you ask that, I realize that it gave me a lot of energy to make the effort to have this birthday party. That is a bit surprising to me. I hadn't really thought about it that way." The conversation continued with the alternative story being able to gain enough significance to stand alongside the original, more problematic story. The problematic story lost its ability to *fully* define the experience of the care seeker, and that is the goal of narrative listening. The key to doing this kind of listening is always to be alert to those gaps and exceptions residing in the problem-filled story so that they can be included in the reflective response.

Narrative Questioning

Narrative questioning is used in conjunction with double listening. Simply stated, narrative questioning consists of questions that are asked in the service of inviting, empowering, and enriching the alternative story (alternative to the problem-filled story). Narrative questions are used to help distance the problem from the person (in the externalizing aspect of narrative listening) or to further invite and strengthen the alternative story being told. So in the previous example, when the care companion asks, "What was it like to offer that gift of a party to your grandson?" they are asking the care seeker to relive their experience of making a choice to have the party, to do all the preparation for it, and to reexperience the pleasure of the party. In reliving the experience of a situation that defined them differently than the problem story does, they give significance and meaning to a story that they otherwise might have overlooked. The problem story has had the dominant defining role for them. It is only when the alternative story is strengthened and, thus, made more significant that it is able to broaden the person's view of themselves beyond that offered by the problem-filled story.

Similarly, when the care companion asks the care seeker, "Did it surprise you that you were able to push away your low energy to provide such a great experience for your grandson?" the care seeker experiences a chance to reevaluate the way they have been seeing themselves and offer themselves a new possibility. The care seeker's statement that she got a lot of energy from the experience (rather than losing energy as she had assumed about future entertaining) and that this did surprise her is not an unusual response to this kind of question. People are often pleased and surprised when they reconsider their problem-oriented assumptions about themselves. The question offers the care seeker an opportunity to test out this new view of herself and see if it has staying power for her. Of course, the problem story will be waiting in the wings to take over the defining process again, so it's important that the care companion give the care seeker plenty of opportunities to strengthen this new view of herself. The care companion could ask another question to help strengthen the story, like,

"Would you say this was a good experience or not a good experience?" to allow the care seeker to evaluate the worth of this new sense of self. They might ask even more directly something like, "What does this experience say about who you are?" which offers the care seeker a way to make an overt claim about herself. These kinds of questions encourage a care seeker to build upon a positive sense of self from an otherwise barely noticed alternative experience as well as inviting the person to reclaim an identity that the problem story was covering up.[7]

The key to asking effective narrative questions is to remember why they are being asked and not to rush through them. The purpose of these carefully designed questions, again, is to help a more resource-filled story emerge alongside the problem story. The questions, because neither the one asking them nor the one responding to them automatically knows their answer, invite the care seeker to step inside the experience of the alternative story in order to find an answer to the question. The care companion then can become interested in finding out about that story as fully as possible in order for it to gain enough strength and meaning to survive.

Conclusion

This chapter has offered the reader the key practices that inform lay pastoral care through a narrative lens. The four practices—narrative attitude, narrative presence, narrative listening, and narrative questioning—are anchoring points for an approach to lay care that supports, encourages, and empowers care seekers. They are based in the theories described in chapter 2 and take place in the collaborative framework of training and consultation that will be presented in the next chapter.

They are not simple, nor are they just techniques. They reflect a profound respect and partnership between care companions and care seekers. The next chapter focuses on helping care companions prepare to engage in these important ministries of care.

A QUESTION TO CONSIDER: What would developing and practicing both a narrative attitude and a narrative presence mean for your care ministry, and how is that different from other ways you have thought about lay pastoral care?

4

Collaborative Learning Communities

Primrose Church hopes to enhance their ministry by developing networks of care for congregation members who find themselves needing extra support. Their goal is to develop several ministry teams that can respond to the diverse needs of people who are experiencing situational vulnerabilities such as hospitalizations and illnesses, divorces, death, grief, relational changes, and other acute and short-term challenges. At the same time, they know that some people need support for chronic conditions, such as health issues, relational disruptions, family dynamics, or other kinds of life complexities. By providing care through multiple and diverse networks, the church believes that it can make a difference in the lives of individuals and families. As more people are trained, they bring those skills into their extended social networks and even into the larger community.

As Primrose begins to work toward the creation of these networks, they are clear that they want to build on the narrative principles and practices explored in the previous chapters of this book. While they are not quite sure what steps to take next, they know that the training process is critical to their success. Although no one involved in the leadership for imagining these care networks is trained as a counselor or specialist, they know that whatever tools they draw on in their training must involve educational models that are collaborative and mutual in their engagement. While content is important, they are also aware that the training must convey more than that. Engagement in collaborative conversations, trust building, and deeper self-awareness enhances the learning of concrete practices like careful listening, offering appropriate responses, and asking questions that move toward meaning. In addition, they are eager to theologically reflect on their own beliefs and ask questions in ways that open themselves up to new understandings and experiences of God.

This book is designed for congregations like Primrose that have discerned that lay narrative care can ultimately transform churches and communities. In order to help readers think about training models for such networks, this chapter begins with an exploration of collaborative theory, which supports the commitments and values suggested by narrative care. Shifting the model of care and training to more narrative and collaborative approaches is not simply a change in the theory of counseling and care. Such a shift recognizes that theology lies at the heart of training, education, and the delivery of care in congregations and communities. This chapter points to some of the theological implications of this work.

Learning in Community

The pastoral care model we propose here shifts the orientation of care from one of counseling others toward a consultative model of mutual connections and conversations with persons who experience a need. While this difference may seem subtle, the shift is substantial. Among the more significant aspects of this approach is the shift from experts who counsel persons in need to care companions who invite persons into conversations about concerns of the heart and soul. The one responding to the needs of others is not an advice giver or a counselor (in the traditional sense of that word). Instead, they genuinely join people by listening carefully and asking good questions that help people become more of who they wish to be as they move through difficult moments.

Educational models for learning about narrative care need to support the values and commitments of this approach. Much like narrative theory, collaborative understandings rest in more postmodern visions that are less certain about belief systems, are more open to questions and dialogues, and place stronger value on diversity of thought and unique ways of being. Collaborative learning communities provide the level of deep connection that engenders understanding.

Learning in community provides an intentional, peer-supported context in which to wrestle with narrative commitments, to practice skills, and to reflect on processes together. Collaborative learning emphasizes the importance of dialogue and reflection about previously held certainties and unquestioned truth claims. Learners have an opportunity to ask questions about old ideas and explore biases and assumptions. For example, a belief that God wants us to learn from a challenge we face often surfaces in situations of care. Learning communities invite people to be curious about this assumption rather than simply asserting it to be true or false. Together, we are able to explore alternative perspectives and positions in ways that are not defensive or heavy-handed. We can think out loud with one another without worrying about doing harm to care seekers or attempting to convince vulnerable people that their theology is not "right."

Notions of collaboration have influenced the fields of therapy, pastoral care, leadership, and other disciplines. It is not unusual to hear people suggest that the activity they are involved with—leading a congregation, working on a project, or engaging in problem-solving—is collaborative. Yet there are many viewpoints about what this term means. Some suggest that to be collaborative means that people are working alongside one another, often on parallel tracks, each tackling the same issue from different perspectives. Many computer programs offer opportunities for collaborative thinking as multiple people work on one project, building solutions to problems faced in business or elsewhere. Likewise, teachers and counselors draw on the word *collaborative* to suggest that they are working alongside someone in a common activity. In its most popular usage, the term is a simple recognition that multiple people are working together on a common project. When we use the word *collaborative* in this project, we intend to point toward a deeper and more engaged way of being with one another. Those who self-identify as collaborative therapists or teachers note that something new and unique is created because of the interaction with another. Genuine engagement with others creates something that could not have been accomplished alone or without the benefit of someone else's wisdom. The influence or change might appear to be minor yet is often significant.

Harlene Anderson, one of the leaders in collaborative therapy, suggests a philosophical stance at the heart of collaborative work—"a 'way of being' in relationship and conversation: a way of thinking with, experiencing with, relating with, acting with, and responding with the people we meet."[1] This collaborative work deeply values the personhood, experiences, and wisdom of others as well as one's own. It is intentional and often challenging work, as it does not dismiss the differences that arise as people genuinely engage one another. Yet something deeply relational occurs in collaborative encounters, inviting new visions and ideas that were not present in exactly the same way without the experience.

Collaborative learning communities in pastoral care depend on this deeper and more connected way of engaging peers and colleagues. Communities come together so that they might learn with one another, enhance their skills, and become more effective as care companions in the church. We believe that collectives of individuals, when working out of a narrative framework, provide the kind of connection with one another that can deeply and positively inform the care that is offered in a congregation. In a parallel way, as care companions consult together about pastoral care, they build relationships that support and nurture their care with one another. These mutual relationships enhance the learning process. Training groups where deeper connections occur can begin to shift the paradigm for care from a more clinical perspective, reorienting it toward a narrative vision of deep listening and active engagement.

Implementation of this training model depends on four principles of collaborative learning. First, the collaborative learning groups create a deeply relational space where people care with one another, value their collective wisdom, and learn from one another's experiences and perspectives. Second, the groups function collaboratively, recognizing a shift in the dynamics of power as people understand their role as conversation partners who embrace an attitude of openness. They have neither answers to questions nor specific responses to challenging moments. Third, as the learning communities become places of connection, each care partner continues to learn, growing in their ability to live with ambiguity, while also carrying a stronger sense of agency. Finally, the groups become intentional spaces for theological reflection as people explore their values and belief systems. A look at each of these aspects guides us in our thinking about the importance of these learning communities.

Relational Care

Narrative pastoral care is deeply relational, done not in isolation but in the context of communities. We connect as we reach out, hoping that we can make a difference in another's life. Such care is built on the assumption that both the one offering care and the one receiving care will be changed by the process of engagement. We assume that those in the learning communities genuinely want the best for one another. Collaborative learning supports this work of connection and trust building as these groups become places of genuine, relational care. Care companions learn to care for one another as they also strengthen their pastoral care skills for care seekers. Collaborative learning communities provide the space necessary for developing relationships with one another in ways that matter to each member of the community. Three theoretical concepts—joining, "withness thinking," and relational accountability—provide guidance as learning communities develop a deeper and more expansive relational network of care.

Since pastoral care is never done in isolation, it is important to imagine the various ways that people can join with one another. Joining means that people get to know one another.

They commit to a shared enterprise of learning and care rather than just focusing on helping others. They consult with one another and hold one another accountable for their shared ministry. Of course, in many religious traditions, this concept recognizes that we are also joining the activity of God. In the learning communities of narrative pastoral care, joining occurs as people connect with one another in conversation, reflection, and action. It enriches those engaged in care. Drawing on our curiosity, we enter conversations with one another about what, and who, we are engaging. Underneath this perspective rests an assumption that people yearn for connection, for being known, and for the mutuality of care.

In the collaborative learning environment, peers join in mutual conversation around care situations. Together, group members collaborate with one another while also increasing their capacities for narrative care. They become companions who bring the expertise of listening deeply, asking questions about meaning, inviting narratives and stories that are complex and multilayered, and imagining with peers what unique and life-giving outcomes are possible. In the mutual dialogue among group members, new relationships are formed that make a difference in the life of the community of learners.

The way we join others has an impact not only on those in the learning community but also on those whom we companion. In joining, we do more than show up; rather, we find ways to listen and respond with care, to ask good questions, and to invest in our conversations, knowing that they make a difference. Rather than investing in the problem or a solution, we center on the person we are encountering and bring our curiosity and imagination into the dialogue. The power of care emerges in these interactions. The connection between persons invites a sense that we are not offering care by ourselves, but we are working with each other to reflect on how best to companion others in their journeys.

The metaphor of joining is supported in collaborative theory by terms such as *mutual puzzling* or *co-explorer*, suggesting something about the stances people bring to their conversational work.[2] Meaningful conversations are created as companions encourage their curious natures and seek wisdom with one another, knowing that the dialogue is less about looking for perfect interventions of care and more about listening for life-giving narratives. Such mutuality offers a vision for being and learning *with* others about ways to embody care. As Anderson says, engaging meaningfully with one another creates a "withness process that is intrinsically more participatory and mutual and less hierarchical and dualistic."[3] In these moments, two dynamics occur at the same time. First, care companions are in dialogue with one another about the care they are offering; second, as laypersons join one another in mutual conversation, they create a deeper relational learning community. Ultimately, the care experienced in the learning communities extends to others, having a positive impact on those in the congregation.

To create meaningful community, a sense of relational accountability and transparency must be part of collaborative learning. Those who offer care are accountable not only to those seeking care but to other colleagues in the pastoral care networks. This accountability includes maintaining confidentiality among those in the learning groups as well as with those who are seeking care. Because the training groups are accountable to one another and to those to whom they offer care, developing trust is important. The group is enhanced by honesty and a willingness to engage differences of experience, perspective, or life lessons while offering possibilities for creative imagination and generative conversation. Such deep relationships open up the possibilities for people to speak without fear that they, or their narrative, will be judged or dismissed. As Anderson suggests, one of the goals of collaborative engagement "is in creating a culture in which participants mutually explore and share expertise or knowledge as they strive to understand each other and achieve desired futures."[4] Again, the goal is not to find the "right" response to a situation but to listen deeply, to retain a curious posture, and to open up the realm of possibilities for engaging the narratives that can empower people in their journeys.

Care companions invite forth the best of themselves and one another as they move into conversations. Appropriate structures of support and accountability such as ground rules, record keeping, and consultation increase care companions' transparency with one another and nurture growth in honest and vulnerable ways. The educational model we are proposing values diversity while also knowing that differences can lead to disagreements and conflicts among people. Because knowledge and wisdom are rather fluid and built around experiences of the past and hopes for the future, our understandings about care are diverse. Important for growth in these learning communities is the willingness and the ability to disagree respectfully and learn with one another, even in our disagreements. The practice of participating in a relational community that is diverse positively shapes our capacities for caring with others.

Shifting Power and Knowledge

Collaborative learning communities live in two realities that shift understandings of power and knowledge. First, these groups build on learning models that recognize different kinds of power, embracing educational models that are less hierarchical as they rely on shared power and wisdom. Second, communities of learning value and understand that multiple perspectives are useful in thinking about care. Together, these realities increase a sense of shared power and knowledge that is rich and diverse for both the learning communities and their work as care companions in the congregation. A cursory look at each of these understandings illuminates their importance in the pastoral care modeled in this book.

As we shift the paradigm for care, it becomes clear that both persons in a caring relationship are changed, and both are part of a larger transformative process. Transformation occurs in a fluid and mutual way. The relationship becomes a place where both people experience changes in perspective. The care seeker may offer a perspective about their experience of health or wellness that then invites the care companion to expand their own understanding, thus creating a transformative moment. This more fluid understanding of caregiving is one of mutual relationship and shared power.

This shift to share power has implications for the educational models that support narrative pastoral care. Just as there is no fixed and permanent distinction between caregivers and care receivers, neither is there a fixed difference between teachers and learners. Teaching and learning is a process that requires an appreciation for the fact that teachers are learners, and learners are also teachers. In some educational models, there is little ambiguity about who carries the most expertise in the classroom and who has the most authority. It is true that as teachers trained in a particular field, we carry a wealth of intellectual and experiential knowledge into the classroom. It is also true that those identified as students carry considerable knowledge and expertise gathered from their diverse backgrounds, experiences, and passions. It is not that one has knowledge and the other does not; rather, there are diverse kinds of knowledge, and in collaborative learning environments, each is valued in its particularity. Such diversity of perspectives creates a rich context for learning with and from one another. What has become increasingly clear for many of us who teach is that the traditional understandings of authority and power limit our growth as teachers. When knowledge is understood to be one-sided, the richness of collaborative and relational understanding is lost.

Many current adult educational models build on collaborative learning, believing that people generating knowledge together is particularly valuable. The development of online and in-person communities known as wisdom communities (WisCom) illustrates this shifting educational model. The goal of these learning environments "is to create a wise community that shares a common mission, engages in reflection and dialogue, believes in mutual trust, respect, and commitment, cares for the common good, and empowers its members. The community provides the opportunity for participants to interact, receive feedback, and learn and grow together."[5] In a parallel way, care companions work with one another in ways that are generative for all involved, in part because each person's wisdom and knowledge are valued. Narrative care and collaborative learning value the ways that knowledge is defined. In the past, many churches have relied on teaching models that were driven by expertise in clinical matters such as depression, grief, addictions, and more. In addition, some churches have depended on supervision by specialists in counseling or pastoral care. While these models can be helpful, we are proposing that a distinctive aspect of narrative care is the acknowledgment that those engaged in the care networks bring their own wisdom and knowledge. Strategies for learning need to be consistent with the values of narrative commitments, including the invitation to share collectively the knowledge each one carries. Instead of depending on the transmission of intellectual knowledge, or the knowledge of an expert counselor, our model also values the wisdom people bring from their everyday lives and experiences.

Learning communities that are formed out of shared power and a willingness to learn with one another embody a greater flexibility and a willingness to try on new perspectives, skills, or patterns of conversation. Trusting the generative aspect of collaborative learning communities rests on reminding ourselves that we do not know all there is to know about the individual narratives of those with whom we care. In collaborative learning environments, we come to know one another in new ways while, at the same time, knowing that we do not know the fullness of another person, nor do we know what is best for someone else. This stance nurtures a sense of honest humility and an ability to recognize the gift of uncertainty. It also leads toward the valuing of alternative perspectives and visions. As Anderson suggests, "A conversational partner, who values the other's expertise, who joins in mutual inquiry, and who foregoes the certainty of preformed knowledge, invites and entails uncertainty."[6] This ambiguity should not be understood as negative; rather, we are boldly trusting that uncertainty is part of life, knowing that it can foster a deeper respect for diverse perspectives. Such differences in knowledge generate greater possibilities for creativity in responding to care situations.

Collaborative work in therapy holds "a fundamental trust in clients' ideas about what is best for them. It includes holding a client's views in the highest esteem and using them as cornerstones of our work with clients."[7] In the work of pastoral care, there is a similar dynamic as we recognize the importance of the knowledge that both the care seeker and the care companion bring. The work of collaborative learning communities is built on trusting the wisdom of those involved while not being overly invested in finding a perfect way to care. A genuinely collaborative approach shifts the dynamics and structures of power in the learning relationship as well as in the actual care offered to others.

Increasing Agency in Care Situations

One of the primary outcomes of narrative care is the enhanced agency of the care seeker. However, we also strive to increase agency in care companions through collaborative learning communities. By agency, we mean the ability to take initiative and action on one's own behalf. As care companions learn with one another, they grow in their ability to respond to the care situations they encounter with a sense of openness and increased confidence. A learning environment that functions in a collaborative and collegial way supports competency and invites people to take action in the ministry of care. Three elements in these educational settings encourage care companions to trust themselves more often as they consult with people in situations of care.

First, the collaborative learning environment offers an opportunity for people to try out their skills, to practice taking on new perspectives, and to grow in their ability to engage others with care. Our assumption is that care companions genuinely want to grow in their capacities to join others in the journey of care. We are eager to bring our best selves to the activities of care, and we are willing to be vulnerable in practicing what we are learning with one another. Anderson notes, "Self-agency refers to a sense of competency or ability to perform or take action, to have choices, and to participate in the creation of choices."[8] As care companions work with one another, they increase their sense that they are able to act in ways that are more congruent with their narrative commitments. Among the hopes for the learning communities is that as the care companions participate in the groups, they also gain a stronger perception of the multiple ways to care. Again, the goal is to engage one another's imagination about responses that empower people in the context of care.

We know that trying new ways of engaging people in care entails risk. For example, people often feel self-conscious about new language or responses and sometimes turn to old patterns of thinking or believing. Yet the power of these learning communities is that we can explore multiple responses to a situation or think through a context in new ways. As one educational researcher suggests, "We learn to be humans living in families and communities. Most of what we 'learn' is not taught in any conventional sense."[9] As people engage one another, receiving genuine feedback and offering good questions, the learning communities become a place to learn about what it means to be human and to listen for life-giving stories. The collaborative learning environments provide an opportunity to remain curious, to learn from the experience of responding in new ways, and to explore integrated learning. As noted educational theorist Jane Fried suggests, "People learn most effectively and profoundly when thinking, feeling, acting, and constructing personal meaning."[10] The learning communities become a place to think, feel, act, and construct ways of being that are more narrative and collaborative.

The learning communities also become a place to ask new questions about previous habits and to grow in one's ability to sit in the discomfort of not knowing how to respond to someone, answer a question, or formulate an inquiry. Living with uncertainty and ambiguity invites a willingness to take chances and to be more creative in care situations. And yet, it also invites humility about not having all of the answers. As a result, care companions are less hesitant in their responses, growing more comfortable with knowing that they don't have the answers for someone's challenges yet knowing they do have expertise at inviting forth narratives. Again, the goal is to focus on pastoral conversations, not on assessing or fixing or answering. As people learn with one another, a certain joy emerges as they recognize what others have to offer in their own journey.

Second, as care companions learn new skills and try on new perspectives, they increase their sense of confidence about doing ministry in the care situations they encounter. Experiencing growth in their skills, care companions also become better able to care without constantly wondering if they are doing it "right." The increase in confidence equates not to "knowing more" but to feeling more comfortable joining someone in the care journey without having all the answers. As companions invite and engage in stories, they experience the transformative power of narrative care. Narrative pastoral care nurtures curiosity in care companions as they invite stories that are empowering with care seekers. This ability is grounded in mutual exploration and conversation that can invite narratives that are more life-giving to arise. The action is not one of directing others; rather, it is one of listening deeply and then inviting alternative stories that are part of someone's preferred way of living. Engaging in mutual conversation offers multiple perspectives. This collaborative process of mutual connection and conversation can become not only generative but also life-giving.

Finally, in the learning communities, care companions increase their sense of self-awareness. When learning narrative care, we find that honesty and intentionality are required of us. Those of us who undertake this work begin to recognize some of our own vulnerabilities and strengths. Self-awareness helps us not insert ourselves into the stories of others, thus allowing the care seeker to remain the focus of care. For example, we may begin to see that our tendency to diagnose someone's sadness mirrors something from our own experience or that our attention to family dynamics and eagerness to assess the various systems at play in a family relates to assumptions we carry about family. Coming to understand these parts of our stories and their impact on our care practices with others can be an incredible gift to both the care seeker and care companion.

Care, offered in the context of community, provides an opportunity to come to know ourselves better and to explore our belief systems in new ways. When learning with others, we begin to not only rely on our own way of thinking but draw on the wisdom of the group as we raise new questions or get curious about something we do not understand.

Theological Reflection

The fourth element important to collaborative learning is the invitation to ask theological questions. A primary task of the church and congregational life is that of inviting others to reflect on their understanding of God, human relationships, and the way God acts and participates in the world. The learning communities become intentional spaces for reflection as people ask theological questions or deconstruct and reconstruct their value and belief systems.

In *How to Think Theologically*, Howard Stone and James Duke offer a way of imagining how we move from beliefs that are "embedded" in our histories and in our lives toward a more "deliberative" theology that has been tested and thought through in new ways."[11] We all carry theological beliefs that are part of our histories or faith communities' narratives. For example, many people are challenged by the death of a child. Our embedded theologies about such tragedy can lead to a variety of responses. Or some might suggest that "God needs another angel in heaven" or that "this is part of God's plan." Yet when confronted with such pain as the loss of a child, people often begin to question what they have known or believed to be true. In a collaborative learning environment, we have the opportunity to reflect on and practice a variety of theological options, knowing that it would be inappropriate to invite those in a caregiving situation. Thinking together about our theologies can move care companions toward a more deliberative or reflective way of relating to claims about God.

Such a move toward a deliberative theology is less about naming what is right or wrong about a particular theology; rather, it is an invitation to rethink what we imagined to be "true" about God or human beings or our relationships with one another. Remaining curious about our own beliefs provides the space we need to reimagine and revision our relationships. Engaging in theological conversations in learning groups keeps us from trying to work out our theological beliefs in the midst of someone else's crisis.

Learning communities become places to ask new questions and to wonder about alternative visions of God. As Stone and Duke suggest, everyone is a theologian in their own right. Although most people do not have a theological degree from a seminary, all of us think about the nature of God, what it means to be human, and what encourages healthy and whole relationships. The key to becoming a theologically competent care companion is to invite our theology to continue to grow as we walk alongside others in both our learning and our caregiving. In fact, it is impossible to engage in pastoral care without involving our theological imagination. In the process, we cocreate our theology and reconstruct theologies that are more open and sometimes even more tentative. As we encounter deep suffering and pain, we find ourselves asking urgent questions.[12] As pastoral companions discuss a situation in the context of their learning environment, they will discover that their views differ. For example, some imagine evil to be personalized and alive in the world. Others suggest that sometimes bad things just happen and that God is not an active participant in the harming but is present in the healing. Still others understand God to be an educator, thinking that whatever comes to us "teaches" us something. And some people move quickly to "forgive and forget" as an answer to pain inflicted upon humans by others. The learning communities are not places where we argue about which of these theological positions is in error, or what is the correct way to embrace our convictions. Rather, the learning communities become places to honestly deliberate about how theology makes a difference in our living and in our care with one another. In this context, theological differences are not to be resolved but become places for mutual conversation and expanded ideas.

Participating in the learning communities requires a temporary suspension of what we have come to believe is true as we explore diverse perspectives. This diversity invites theological curiosity that wonders about things more than invests in the answers to them. By not moving toward solving theological questions but engaging them with sincerity and openness, we invite new ways of thinking that we might not have imagined before.

This process of imagination and curiosity involves an openness to questioning the assumptions we bring to our theology. All of us carry some deeply held beliefs that are challenging to examine. In many ways, these belief systems guide our thinking and our practices. The key is not to simply decide some beliefs are better than others but to genuinely engage in the kind of conversation that invites an openness to new ways of thinking about such things as the power of God or the limitations of God or the value or lack of meaning in suffering.

As care companions engage in theological reflection, we want to do all that we can to make sure that the training is thoughtful and connected to the church's theological commitments and visions. We are eager not to reinforce past stances that have created harm, such as an inappropriate use of Scripture or an adamant belief that God is in total control and knows all that is going to happen.

Justice-Making Relationships

A significant theological commitment worthy of our reflection is that of promoting justice. Both narrative and collaborative theories have a theological congruence with principles of justice. While the term *justice* has many definitions, we understand it to be concerned with the flourishing and wholeness of individuals while promoting the common good for all of humanity. When we work toward justice, we pay attention to how relationships are developed and embodied, recognizing power imbalances where they exist and honoring the agency of others to make choices for their lives. As participants in the networks of care, we embrace justice in our relationships with one another and with care seekers.

Pastoral care has always been committed to wholeness in people's lives, especially amid suffering, oppression, hopelessness, or despair. Until recently, we have understood these values to be individually significant in our care with one another, but we have been less adept at thinking about how structural and systemic injustice—whether intentional or unintentional—jeopardizes the common good for all people. We have come to see that individual wholeness is connected to the flourishing of all human beings. Many theological scholars, particularly those who are committed to liberative practices, pay attention to how oppression, marginalization, powerlessness, exploitation, and systemic violence mark everyday lives.[13] Pastoral care providers understand that confronting systems of oppression such as racism, classism, sexism, heterosexism, and other structures that inhibit wholeness is part of the complexity of care. As pastoral theologian Nancy Ramsay points out, such a focus in our care examines social inequality and the dynamics of power and "prioritizes constructive, politically informed engagement to promote the wellbeing of all God's people, regardless" of political status, religious belief systems, class privilege, or marginalization.[14]

Justice-making in narrative care and collaborative learning builds on three components that operate together:

deconstructing cultural norms, storytelling that empowers, and standing in solidarity.

Deconstructing Cultural Norms

We live in a world where the definition of *normal* is narrow and prescribed. The world around us encourages us to imagine that there is a standard we ought to live up to in our personal and professional lives, alongside specific expectations about what it means to be healthy or smart or good. Most often, these norms are reinforced in both overt and subtle ways. For example, when children are born, the culture assigns them a gender that we assume will orient them to the world. Those around the child relate to them through this gender identity, suggesting there are some things boys do (such as provide leadership) while there are other things reserved for girls (such as provide good care). Such normative thinking shapes the way a child experiences herself or himself, diminishing the fullness of that child. These messages become part of a dominant self-understanding, keeping people from exploring all of the possible options for their lives.

As discussed earlier, narrative care invites stories that help people discern for themselves what it means to be whole and to flourish. The most dominant cultural story is deconstructed as care seekers begin to tell stories that have sometimes been implicit in their self-perceptions. In training programs, as care companions relate to one another, they remain attentive to stories that counter problematic cultural norms, resulting in a greater confidence about offering care to others. For example, someone may discover that they have a stronger ability to think analytically than they previously imagined, possibly because of cultural stereotypes placed upon them. However, in the context of a learning community, they are affirmed for their emerging skills, and they begin to risk speaking up more boldly in the group. Greater justice-making is possible when we resist those cultural norms that function to keep people in their places or that diminish their well-being and connection to others. The invitation to be true to one's own sense of self is, indeed, countercultural as people begin to resist norms that are placed on them, finding ways to embrace identities of their own choosing.

Storytelling That Empowers

Inviting people to tell their own stories in ways they prefer also supports their sense of agency, defined as the ability to act on one's own behalf. This process empowers people and is a critical element in a justice-making relationship. We especially invite the stories in people's lives that remind them of their resiliency, strengths, resources, and hopes, thus countering a sense that they are somehow deficient or less than. For example, in a learning environment, we might see that the way someone is responding to a situation characterizes a new way of relating for them. By asking them how they knew to respond in this way, we affirm their agency to make new choices in conversations. They might have seen a peer in the group respond to a care seeker with a sense of empathy in a situation they would have found challenging to navigate. They can't imagine they would have known how to respond as their peer did. However, after seeing someone else demonstrate empathy in a training meeting, they may try out some similar responses. Although the words they use or the intonation in the conversation may not yet feel comfortable to them, they might also find the person they are listening to responds positively to their conversation. Hence instead of thinking they don't know how to respond, they come to see that they can engage someone in a new way, and they are interested in trying it again.

While this illustration may seem simple, it demonstrates how changing the storytelling about ourselves can activate our agency in positive ways. When we invite stories about strengths we carry, rather than just the problems that are getting in our way, we counter the negative, deficit-oriented thinking that often keeps us from experiencing greater joy or peace. Inviting stories of strength functions as justice-making in our relationships because it encourages us to prioritize our possibilities rather than our limits.

Standing in Solidarity

Justice-making requires that we stand with others in their journeys, especially with those who are on the margins or who experience less power in our world. The most vulnerable people deserve our strongest allyship. To stand with someone means that we take seriously their experiences of feeling marginalized because of their religion, gender, orientation, age, or any other quality. We also recognize that we cannot speak for others, but we can invite people to tell their own stories in their own words. We walk carefully as we practice our care and encourage others to use their voices, supporting them in the process.

As we become aware of the complexity of people's situations, we are often reminded about our relative position of privilege or power. For example, seeing someone suffer from the loss of employment while we work in jobs or careers that are meaningful may lead us to feel guilty or attempt to make the other person feel better. Or knowing that the medical care someone needs is more than their minimal insurance will pay for may prompt us to try to fix the situation without turning to other systems for support. When we become aware of others' vulnerabilities, we might have the experience of standing on sacred or holy ground as people share the details of their lives. We also might have feelings of loss, confusion, anger, or guilt because of our own experience of relative power. Religious educator Katherine Turpin suggests that as we come to self-awareness about our privilege, we often have characteristic responses such as trying to fix problems, turning to guilt and despair, or trying to neutralize our anger. She suggests these are times when we need instead to listen to multiple voices, embrace conflict in positive ways, and remain open in the process by drawing on spiritual resources.[15] In justice-making relationships, we do not dismiss or deny differences; rather, we recognize the complexity of our lives and seek to stand with others in solidarity.

Justice-making in our ministry teams and with care seekers is critical to the work we are called to do. Paying attention to how we build relationships in our congregations can lead the church to be a stronger instrument of justice in the world.

A QUESTION TO CONSIDER: What does creating a collaborative learning environment mean, and how can you further develop that in your own pastoral care learning process?

5

CURRICULAR POSSIBILITIES FOR LAY CARE GROUPS

So far, in this book, we have tried to articulate a dynamic, multilayered model of lay pastoral care in congregations. This approach has several unique aspects. First, it offers a model of caregiving that, although based on a therapeutic theory (narrative therapy), seeks to provide a structure for supportive and empowering care that is not oriented toward a traditional counseling approach or even toward traditional pastoral listening but rather suggests a consultative empowerment model between companion and care seeker. Second, it promotes multiple layers of care and connection within the congregation, operating under the premise that the more people who are invited and trained in pastoral care, the more the whole congregation will connect with and support one another. And third, it is based in collaborative learning communities that, in and of themselves, become environments for spiritual growth, self-knowledge, and enriched relationships among the group members and beyond. These three dimensions are intended to both facilitate the support of people in transitions, crises, or isolation and enrich the spiritual and relational well-being of the congregation. Creating this kind of enlivening, synergistic energy for the whole congregation is as important as the training process for the individual care teams.

This chapter offers curricular ideas and teaching/learning methods for this model of lay pastoral care by looking at a specific congregation where I, Christie, used this approach as a pilot program. This case study is not intended to be prescriptive. Each congregation will have its own needs, priorities, and resources for developing a lay pastoral care program. In addition, the case study will focus on just one of the several care groups in this congregation, the parish companions, because they took on the most complex care needs and, thus, received the most training. Curricular ideas and learning processes for other care groups from this congregation will also be explored but not to the same extent.

Pilot Program Case Study

This congregation is a medium-sized United Methodist church in the outer rings of a city in the upper Midwest. It is an established congregation dating back over one hundred fifty years. Many families in the church have ancestors who were part of the original congregation, but also many people from the neighborhood and elsewhere have joined more recently. The average age of the membership is late sixties, although there is a good representation of all ages. The congregation is relatively financially stable. The church would be considered more on the progressive side of the theological spectrum, although not all members would locate themselves there. This is an active and involved congregation that supports a food shelf, offers programs to the families in the neighborhood on a regular basis, provides a thrift shop, participates in housing homeless families in rotation with other city churches, and supports various programs of social justice. It has an active music program (including offering college scholarships to young people majoring in music) and well-respected musicians and choir. Multiple enrichment groups in the congregation include women's and men's support groups, Bible study groups, book groups, a lunch-and-learn group for older members, and various shorter-term educational offerings. The staff includes a senior pastor, a part-time family ministry pastor, a part-time parish nurse, a part-time music director / organist plus two paid part-time musicians, a communications / front office person, a bookkeeper, and building maintenance people. It also has a well-established day care center with a director and several teachers who are on the church's payroll. Although this church has multiple staff and ample resources, the development of lay care programs like this is not dependent on those factors. We have worked with a number of smaller congregations with fewer staff that have developed similar lay care programs.

I (Christie) became involved in this church when, in my role as a pastoral care professor, I was invited to consult with the staff-parish relations committee about a situation in the congregation. I was impressed by the vitality of the church and also by its hospitality. My husband and I had been looking for a new congregation, and we began to attend this church. The senior pastor at the church, seeking to revitalize the congregation, was especially interested in developing three aspects of church life: deepened spiritual growth (offered through Wesleyan-type small groups), a more enlivened sense of community within the whole congregation, and a well-developed lay pastoral care program that would contribute to both the other goals. She asked the newly hired parish nurse to coordinate the pastoral care program and asked me to be both consultant and teacher.

We, along with a group of interested laypeople, formed a commission to consider the best way to create a vital pastoral care program. We developed a template for a program that would create and train multiple groups (at different levels of training) to offer care in a variety of situations. We had inherited two groups—the Care Ministers and the Parish Ministers. The Care Ministers had initially been recruited to individually partner with a congregant who was unable to physically participate in the life of the congregation. They were to make visits and share news of the church, bring appropriate resources (devotional material, bulletins, newsletters, and the like), and provide a connection to the larger congregation. Group members met together periodically for encouragement and support. They had been functioning under the supervision of the associate minister, who had just left the congregation, and they had lost some direction and focus. Although they continued to meet, they had stopped making regular visits. They were still partnered with care seekers but maintained contact mostly through cards and occasional telephone calls. They had some training that had been conducted early in the group's life.

The Parish Ministers, on the other hand, were actively functioning. For the most part, they were the remnants (with some additions) of a Stephen Ministries group that had disbanded some years prior. Their primary function was to visit people in the hospital. Individually, they were on call one week out of every two months. When on call, they would go to the hospital when someone from the congregation was facing surgery, illness, or other problems. They were directed to go visit as quickly as possible after receiving notification of the hospitalization from the church. This visit didn't take the place of one by the pastor and/or the parish nurse, but it provided an additional connection to the congregation.

The template we developed included a revised version of both the Care Ministers and the Parish Ministers with proposed training through regular group meetings for each. In addition, we listed the hospitality teams—funeral hospitality, Common Threads (who knit prayer shawls for congregants facing challenges), prayer chain volunteers, and so forth—as part of the overall pastoral care program. We considered creating lay-led grief groups (potentially using a trained leader and an apprentice coleader so we could eventually have a pool of trained grief group leaders). This was our starting structure, and we began to put it in place by extending specific invitations to supplement the Parish Ministers and a more general invitation for those interested in other care ministries. We developed curriculum as well as mission statements and "Policy, Procedures, and Practices"[1] documents for most of these groups, initially meeting monthly with each team. The parish nurse coordinated the program (maintaining records and other structures of accountability as well as providing follow-up for any congregant who needed it and any necessary resources and referrals). As coordinator, she has been and continues to be the linchpin of our program. I served as lead consultant and teacher. The senior pastor met regularly with the parish nurse, thus providing oversight for the program.

One other key piece was to introduce the lay care network to the whole congregation as a dynamic concept—that people might serve as a care companion over a period of time, but at some other time, they might be a care seeker. This approach to lay pastoral care didn't place one group of people in the "healthy" position and another group of people in the "needy" position but rather promoted a congregational model of mutual care. We also talked with the congregation—through announcements in church, commissioning rituals, and newsletter articles—about our commitments to appropriate ethics and boundaries, especially our commitment to confidentiality. Names and identifying qualities would not be used in our groups, and only the parish nurse and the consultant would know who were currently care seekers in the programs. We also issued an open-ended invitation to any congregants who felt called to serve in a care ministry role.

Over time, we have revised our program, recognizing that regular evaluation is a crucial part of the process. We discovered we could not identify enough potential grief group participants at any given time to justify the grief groups, and we could recommend a different bereavement resource to our congregants. We added a group called "Soul Food," whose members were on call for one month at a time to provide three days of dinners to people in transition or crisis (new baby, surgery, illness, grief, and so forth). We also added a communion team who would take communion quarterly to people who couldn't get to church. During the Covid-19 shutdown, we added a team we named "Called to Care" whose mission was to maintain telephone and card connections with all members of the congregation while the church campus was closed.

Most significantly, we added a group called "Parish Companions" who were charged with offering one-on-one regular companionship to people who were undergoing a significant reorienting transition, such as receiving a new diagnosis, dealing with a runaway child, working through a divorce, becoming a new primary caregiver for a family member, experiencing a significant loss, and the like. They were tasked with maintaining a ministry of narrative presence and narrative listening for up to one year (with occasional exceptions) with the congregant in transition.

As with the earlier groups, curricular ideas and policy manuals were developed for each program as appropriate. For example, the Soul Food team gathered for an orientation around policies and procedures, including issues of boundaries, confidentiality, and assessment. They had a single session with the intention of meeting annually or, as new teams developed, for a refresher. We did a training session for each new home communion team. The Care Ministers Team met monthly for the first year, when the training was more intense, and then quarterly for support and consultation.

On the other hand, the Parish Companions met monthly for a year before being assigned a companion and continued to meet monthly throughout their tenure as Parish Companions. As new members joined the Parish Companions, we decided to do an intensive training session with them, focusing on ethics, boundaries, confidentiality, and narrative listening. They were then brought into the group to learn with and from the ongoing group members and to be assigned a mentor from within the group for the first year. We will discuss specific curriculum and learning processes later on, but the primary mission of the Parish Companions team was to visit with people in major life transitions and accompany them through the changes necessitated by the situation. They learned how to invite and receive the story the care seeker wished to tell and to help them tell that story in ways that were empowering (using a narrative therapy framework).

The Parish Companions team has now been working together for over six years. We have added members to the team (in groups of three or four) twice over that period of time, and we have lost a few members to death or illness. The group meets monthly for about two hours—checking in with one another, sharing their experiences of ministry visits (using rules of confidentiality), and having conversations that help build skills, develop spiritual and theological insight, and offer support and encouragement. They have provided many hours of companionship to congregants in transition, and they have also been transformed in their own lives and relationships. They often comment that what they have learned in the group has radically changed the ways they relate to others in their lives. They share with one another in the group meetings in ways they rarely share elsewhere because of the trust levels they have developed. In the midst of learning how to care for others, they have learned to care for one another and for themselves in amazing new ways, which is part of the multilayering that is central to these programs.

Curricular Ideas

The key to the curriculum for lay care groups is that it emerges from the needs and interests of the learning communities themselves. The curricular topics are explored in multiple ways, not only in a formal presentation but through consultation about visits and reflections on group interactions. We will explore these ways of developing teaching and learning processes in the next section. It's important, though, to note that while the word *curriculum* might suggest a set of fixed topics to be presented by an expert to a group of students, this is not the primary way learning occurs for these teams. The development of the curriculum is much more consultative and spontaneous than the word might suggest.

Ground Rules

When a pastoral care group like the Parish Companions begins, the first few sessions are about developing a sense of identity, purpose, ground rules, and direction. Through collaborative conversation, we reflect on what we are preparing to do as lay caregivers and why we want to do that work. We explore ideas about what qualities, skills, and commitments we might need in order to do the kind of congregational care that seems most fitting and helpful. We do some self-exploration about what particular gifts and skills we bring to this work and what we hope to learn from one another to develop new skills and attitudes. And we begin to generate the types of ground rules we would like to put in place to help make our learning community as safe, effective, and meaningful as possible. Those ground rules might include the ways we make room for, encourage, and hold one another appropriately accountable. They might include agreements about how to prioritize the work of the group through attendance and focus. They might include ways we can specifically enhance our own and one another's learning, knowing that not all people learn in the same ways. And they always include a commitment to keep these ground rules dynamic—identifying ways that they will be regularly revisited and evaluated and changed as the group develops. The group, including the coordinator and the consultant, join in these important conversations together.

Ethics and Boundaries

Naturally evolving out of these early conversations are ideas especially about the way we will understand and live out our ethical commitments and boundaries in the group and in our work as parish companions. These conversations can take many forms, but we always explore what confidentiality means in both the group setting and the parish companion visits. We look at the difference between confidentiality and secrecy. We talk about confidentiality as part of good boundary keeping and as a way to hold a person's story in the highest respect, always making sure that the care seeker maintains all the storytelling rights to their narrative. We also talk about exceptions to confidentiality, like discussing pastoral visits in the consultation group (without names or other identifying information) and sharing important feedback with the program coordinator, especially if concerns arise from the visit. We also agree about what confidentiality means in the context of our learning community itself. This exploration of confidentiality is crucial to the development of a lay care program, because nothing destroys congregational confidence in a program like this faster than a fear that people's private experiences are going to become exposed to gossip or even well-meaning curiosity. Maintaining confidentiality is essential to lay caregiving programs, and learning how to keep confidences begins in the care team group itself.

Other aspects of the ethics conversation include what it means to maintain appropriate boundaries in our care relationships, including the relational dynamics of time, touch, personal sharing, and so forth. These discussions about confidentiality, boundaries, and relational dynamics are introductory in nature and find their way into almost every group meeting from these early sessions forward. They surface in later groups, not usually in formal presentation, but in consultative conversations about visits or even through interactions in the group itself.

Paradoxes of Care Relationships

The other conversation that naturally evolves out of these early "ground rule" discussions is the focus of future curriculum—what we want and need to learn together. These discussions guide the topics we plan for the presentation portions of our group time and that find their way into more informal conversations in the group. Over the first year of group meetings, some predictable topics arise beyond those of ethics and boundaries. We begin by looking at some of the fundamental paradoxes of pastoral care. For example, we want to be helpful, and yet the best kind of help we can offer is our presence and our careful listening/witnessing to the stories the care seeker wishes to tell. The almost overwhelming "instinct" of lay caregivers is to give advice or try to fix the situation, to take the pain or anxiety or problem away from the care seeker. So we talk about the importance of what might be called "compassionate detachment"—deep presence and focus on what the care seeker is saying as they make meaning out of their situation and also a detachment from the need to guide the care seeker toward a solution the companion sees as desirable. This push/pull between a relational commitment to the care seeker and a detachment from guiding, advising, or solving is one of the most persistent topics for a lay pastoral care group and one of the most difficult to internalize.

Another paradox might be the need to experience compassion or sympathy (processing others' feelings through our own experience) while knowing that empathy (entering another's point of view as much as possible) is much more useful than sympathy and should take on much greater significance in the care relationship. A third paradox might assert a commitment to knowing that God is present in all pastoral relationships even though there may be no "God conversation" during the visit. Discussing these and other pastoral care paradoxes helps lay care companions begin to explore the complexity of care relationships and the need for intentionality in care conversations.

Single and Double Listening

Another predictable curriculum topic that arises early in the first year but continues in one form or another through the life of the learning community is the work of single and double active listening (discussed in chapter 3). Although care companions certainly focus on learning the principles and practices of active listening, the real work comes through discussing how it operates during a visit, noticing how it is used in the general group conversations, practicing it with one another around the table and in paired conversations, reflecting on what happened when it works well and when it doesn't in a visit, offering feedback to one another, and so on.

These four themes—ground rules, ethics and boundaries, the paradoxes of pastoral relationships, and single and double listening—make up an ongoing curriculum that is always part of the care team's learning process.

Larger Curricular Categories

Three additional curricular categories are central to the care teams: the practical, the pastoral, and the spiritual/theological. These broad categories speak to three key dimensions in lay care programs, each serving to enhance both the experience of the care companion as well as that of the care seekers in the congregation.

Practical Issues

In the practical category, we address the kinds of issues that weigh heavily on new parish companions' minds. This would include the nuts and bolts of making a first phone call to set up the time for a visit, starting a pastoral conversation, determining how much time to spend in a visit, preparing for a visit, and so on. As companions gain experience, additional practical issues emerge, such as what to do if a care seeker gives the companion a gift or how to respond when a care seeker wants to complain about the pastor or someone else in the congregation. Practical issues are often a formal part of the early curriculum and then surface more spontaneously as time goes on. Conversations about particular practical matters are always valuable in and of themselves, but often, they point toward more significant issues (like boundaries or ethics concerns) that serve the whole group well.

Pastoral Issues

The pastoral category of curriculum includes those topics that inform the work of pastoral care. These topics are generated by the visits the care team is making. There are certainly some materials that we can predict will be needed by group members. For example, we always include both presentations and discussions on the dynamics of loss and grief, using materials that are in keeping with narrative ideas.[2] Thus, we are more likely to talk about grief through the notion of continuing relationships between the one who has died and the ones who grieve than we are to talk about it as a set of stages or working through unfinished business. Although discussions about loss and grief tend to focus on the loss of a person through death (because this is the context we are most often encountering), we also explore other losses, such as those that occur with unemployment, a runaway child, worsening symptoms of Alzheimer's disease, or a divorce in the family. We might also talk about loss in the context of positive events, such as the graduation of a child from high school, a promotion at work, or a move to a new city. While we may discuss the broader contours of grieving, the particulars of it are always related to the experiences care companions are having in their visits. We learn together how not to make broad assumptions about the way a care seeker experiences their loss and grief or to assume that we have any expert knowledge about the way they will go about making meaning out of their crisis.

Talking about loss and grief may well guide us to other related topics. Depending on the situation, we may want to talk about the experience of dementia or Alzheimer's disease. Or we may explore some ways that people move through relational separation or divorce and different cultural perspectives on those. We might talk about cultural variations in the processing of grief or some cultural considerations of how meaning is made in times of loss. The point here is that while we would almost always include material on loss and grief using narrative-compatible frameworks, more specific conversations will come out of the needs, knowledge, and experiences of the group members.

The same principle would apply to the topic of aging. We might present some of the more common experiences and needs of folks as they enter later life, acknowledging the immense variety of people's aging processes, but the specifics of those conversations would relate to what care team members are encountering in their visits. In this way, we avoid the tendency to draw universal conclusions about how to offer care in situations of aging (or in any situation) and to help companions look to the care seeker for how to understand their experience.

Other pastoral care topics become part of the learning agenda as the group encounters new experiences. Often, the most productive learning comes from a group member's request for help with a particular issue they have encountered in their visits. All group members, including the coordinator and the trainer, are invited to share their own experiences, not in a prescriptive way but in the hopes of generating collaborative knowledge that is fitting to this particular situation. These conversations might include reflections on how to move from casual conversation to a more intentional one or how to invite storytelling that includes a deceased loved one as an active presence in the room. They might involve discussing forms of life review for a person in their later years or how to know when sitting in silence is the most appropriate pastoral act. They might include a personal issue, such as a reluctance to end a care relationship or an uncertainty about what the relationship might look like after the formal care connection is ended. The point is that the best learning for care groups, once the foundations of ethics and boundaries are set and the skills of single and double listening have been introduced, is always contextual and in response to questions and concerns of the moment. In our opinion, a fixed curriculum that tries to present answers to lay caregivers before they have any questions is not a useful approach. Narrative theory gives preference to collaborative learning over the presentation of "expert" knowledge. All group members are invited to be consultants and teachers to one another, and the pastoral care curriculum emerges in this process.

Spiritual and Theological Issues

The third curricular area we named earlier is the spiritual/theological. Attending to the spiritual and theological aspects of both companion visits and personal growth is as important as the practical and pastoral aspects. As we discussed in chapter 4, the work in the care teams often helps group members shift their theological thinking from embedded to deliberative. This happens in at least three ways.

First, in making visits, care companions may be exposed to spiritual perspectives that are different from the ones they have carried. Many times, care companions don't have to question some of their own spiritual assumptions until they have encountered a different point of view. They are committed to carefully listening to the care seeker's story, including the spiritual and theological perspectives within it, so they are usually able to separate their own beliefs from those of the care seekers they visit. They may want to argue, persuade, or contradict as they listen, but their commitment to careful listening and to supporting the care seeker's storytelling rights helps them resist that temptation. However, care companions can share their experience in the group meeting, asking for consultation about the potential contradictions between their assumed beliefs and what they heard in the visit. They might be concerned about something as simple as a spiritual cliché that they have heard ("God doesn't give us more than we can bear") or as complex as multiple understandings of God's role in a crisis ("I don't understand why God is punishing me" alongside "I know this is part of God's plan").

Group members, as they consult with one another about their own, usually embedded spiritual points of view begin to think through their theologies more intentionally. They may recognize that they are uncomfortable with what they have heard and need to explore how their own beliefs conflict with those of the care seeker. Sometimes, what they have heard in the care seeker's story is revelatory in a challenging but positive way. Sometimes, it serves as a tool for clarifying a deeply held theological commitment that they only vaguely understood before. The group conversation helps the care companion sort through their thoughts and feelings, and this process results in a more deliberative theological orientation. This, in turn, helps the care companion feel more secure in their theological commitments (and coincidentally, less rigid in them) so that they can be present to a care seeker's theology in a more focused and supportive way.

As the care companion consults with the group about their theological encounters and reflects on what that means for their own beliefs, the rest of the group members are invited through the process to consider their own theological commitments. They also reflect on what they believe, furthering this move from embedded to deliberative theological reflection. Thus, they also grow in their capacity to understand themselves theologically and spiritually and to encounter multiple points of view without defensiveness or distraction, making them more effective in their pastoral care visits.

A second way group members tend to their own theological and spiritual growth is through intentional encounters with books or articles, reading and discussing them together. For example, a group may read an article on the nature of prayer and find themselves in a lively discussion on how they personally experience prayer in their own faith lives. Or they may read a book about theodicy (God's role in times of crisis and hurt—or why God permits evil) and explore their own images of and beliefs about God. Many accessible resources can help care companions explore what they have believed over time as well as newer ideas that may become part of their spiritual lives.

It is important that during these discussions, group members practice the skills that they have learned about careful listening and rely on the group ground rules about respect, confidentiality, and support. They, hopefully, have developed significant trust in one another through the collaborative learning processes they have employed throughout their group meetings so they can feel comfortable having these somewhat vulnerable conversations about their faith practices. And of course, group members can share at the levels that are comfortable for them and are never pressured to say more than they want to.

Finally, a third way that theological reflection may take place in a group is through the spiritual practices they use as part of the group process. Groups might open with a meditation that finds its way into their later discussion. They might ask for prayers from one another and/or pray together. They might talk about issues in their own lives and vocations that invite spiritual reflection. These and other intentional and spontaneous practices may well enhance the spiritual and theological lives of the group members. Whatever shape they may take, spiritual and theological reflection and growth are essential components of lay pastoral care training.

Shaping a Learning Community

We have discussed previously what we might loosely call "curriculum" for a lay training group. Hopefully, we have made it clear that curriculum, for the most part, emerges out of the care companions' group process rather than being thought of as a "body of knowledge" that needs to be imparted to group members. Several questions remain. How do we invite a group process that best supports this kind of collaborative learning, one that draws on the experience and wisdom of group members rather than relying primarily on designated expert knowledge? How do we generate shared ownership of the group mission and the skills and practices that are most likely to serve that mission? How does the facilitator of the learning group create a structure and process to help the care team best prepare itself without jeopardizing the commitment to collaborative and cooperative learning?

We have generally found that the more group members shape their own learning experience, the better the group functions and the more likely it is to meet the desired learning outcomes. You can see this process at work in our earlier discussion about the way group members begin their work together. They collaboratively define the mission of the group, identify the skills and knowledge needed to fulfill that mission, and set the ground rules that make sure the group will most likely have a positive experience. Those definitional and foundational discussions take place in the early months of the group's life, although they continue to be reshaped and redefined throughout. But as those structuring conversations give way to more reflection on the practical, pastoral, and spiritual dimensions of pastoral care, a process needs to emerge that continues to foster collaborative learning. As much room as possible should be created for shared reflection and discussion, and although leader-driven presentations are necessary, they need to be de-centered in the overall group experience. For the leader, the same theory and skills that guide our approach to caregiving (narrative attitude and presence, narrative listening, and narrative questioning) are the essence of group facilitation. Consequently, we have found that group sessions with the following shape seem to offer the best opportunities for shared discussion and consultation while making the best use of everyone's experience, including that of the leader.

Gathering

Important to any group meeting, especially in a collaborative learning environment, is the gathering. Group members are invited to begin sessions by creating a hospitable environment. People greet one another spontaneously, engaging in the kind of casual conversation that provides gentle relational connections. And as the group begins to settle in, a member of the group invites the rest into an opening meditation, poem, or other reading that serves to recall the group's sense of shared mission. Group members may reflect on what has been shared or just sit with the experience.

Checking In

This opening leads quite naturally into a time when group members check in with one another about what is going on in their lives, especially since they last met. The group, in keeping with their ground rules, is usually conscious of both the time restrictions and the importance of making room for each group member to share, so each person's check-in is generally brief. However, if a person needs a bit more time because of a special situation, the group honors that need. As each person shares, the rest of the group members respond with attentive presence and careful listening.

Consultation about Visits

The most intensive learning times happen when group members talk about their care visits. At each meeting, all members who are currently in a care relationship talk with the group about how the visits are going, focusing on the most recent visit. They do this as anonymously as possible, withholding identifying information and names. After sharing the dynamics of the visit, the companion consults with group members about any questions and concerns they might have. The group generally explores whatever the presenter wishes to focus on. For example, one care companion in a group with which I consult talked about her concern that the conversations she was having with the care seeker stayed at the surface level, a more casual conversation, for most of the visit. She noted that the exception to this was after a closing prayer when the care seeker would share more deeply about her concerns. The group discussed this, primarily by asking questions, which resulted in the care companion drawing two important conclusions. First, she realized that she was carrying expectations about what a "meaningful" conversation should look like and that the care seeker was entitled to have whatever conversation she wished to have without pressure to be "deep." Second, she noted that since the prayer seemed to provide a vehicle for the care seeker's concerns and the care seeker seemed to want to share those concerns in that context, it might be helpful for the companion to suggest prayer earlier in the conversation, maybe even as an opening blessing. The next meeting, she reported that both of these strategies (relaxing her own expectations and moving the prayer nearer to the beginning of the visit) seemed to help the care seeker in sharing her story. In another consultation time, the care companion struggled with how to navigate the ending of a care relationship and a return to a simple congregational connection. Through the group feedback, the companion was able to draw on ideas about the caregiving role and relevant boundaries. The consultation brought her both a decision and a sense of confidence. Such examples demonstrate how important consultation time is for learning.

Presentation

Usually, two other segments are included in the care companions' group meetings—a time of presentation and a time of practicing. Presentations come out of group-identified topics about which they would like more formally presented ideas. The presenter, who might be a member of the group or an outside resource, prepares those segments and tries to offer them in ways that allow the group to dialogue with the material rather than just accept it as expert knowledge. The presentations might address topics named earlier in this chapter: dynamics of aging, loss and grief, family life cycle changes, personal and family dynamics around dying, and so forth. The presentation addresses the issue in ways that are consistent with narrative theory in that they are focused on the contexts and values of the people experiencing these events rather than on any universal or general "truths" about them. The hope is that care companions use these materials to help them listen in ways that in turn help the care seeker tell their story in the most meaningful and helpful ways. The group discussions of these presentations are, in our opinion, more helpful than the presentations themselves, because they help group members put the ideas into the contexts of the care visits they are making.

Practice

The other important work in the care groups comes through practicing. This time is primarily focused on the four narrative practices discussed in chapter 3, especially narrative listening and narrative questioning. There are many ways to practice these skills. We generally have someone (often the facilitator) role-play a care seeker who is engaged with a care companion. Then the group can take turns practicing listening responses, either offering single active-listening responses to the care seeker's story or allowing each group member more extended time for conversational give-and-take before shifting the focus to another member.

Since the arrival of the Covid-19 pandemic, most care groups in congregations have had to shift to using technology for their meeting times. This has required new learning for everyone in the group, especially regarding ways to have free-flowing conversation when each person is seen in a little box on a screen rather than face-to-face around a table. Practice time has been especially challenging, but groups have figured out how to imagine themselves around the table and respond accordingly. Since most care visits have also had to be made through technology, computer or telephone, it is fitting that group members have had to find ways to connect with one another as they were trying to find ways to best connect with their care seekers.

Ending a Session

Care group consultation sessions tend to end the way they began, by sharing a reading or a blessing and gently disconnecting with one another through casual conversations. Sometimes a group might spend time discussing how they experienced that session, especially if something unique or intense has occurred. But generally, group members are content to end the group with a blessing because the discussions throughout the session have served as both a consultation for and an evaluation of the group meeting.

The shape of a care group session makes room for the important learning we hope occurs for lay care participants. They build community with one another, deepen their spiritual and relational lives, develop the practices that enhance their care work and generate confidence in that ministry, and build a sense of personal and shared vocation. A session also lays the foundation for individual and group accountability as its members engage in peer consultation for the work of congregational care. It also keeps important lines of communication open, allowing the facilitator and/or coordinator to know what follow-up for either group members or care seekers should be pursued. Each group in a congregational care team network is unique and will find its own shape over time. And different care teams will require different learning agendas and processes depending on the kind of care they are providing.

Other Potential Care Groups

We have focused so far on the care team (Parish Companions) that provides support for people going through crises and major transitions—a group that meets more often and has more extensive learning needs than other groups might. But congregations might want to set up other types of groups with their own learning processes. Each congregation wishing to develop a system of lay care teams needs to assess what is most needed in their particular context, remembering that there are three goals:

- To involve a significant portion of the congregation in a dynamic pastoral care network that enriches the congregation's overall well-being.
- To create care teams that are able to meet the needs of congregants in the various circumstances that may arise.
- To create learning communities that provide both effective training appropriate to the group's mission and support and enrichment for the group members.

In addition to the Parish Companion team that we have focused on in this chapter, congregations might choose to create other kinds of care groups.

CARE GROUPS FOR PEOPLE WITH LIMITING CONDITIONS

This is a group whose members care for congregants who are unable to attend worship because of physical or other kinds of limiting conditions. Members provide regular visits for care and connection, vehicles of communication between the care seeker and the congregational community, and a starting place for matching congregant needs with potential referrals and resources.

Members of this group might also serve home communion to people who can't get to worship services. In that case, the group would need at least one or two sessions to talk about the nuances of at-home communion and how to share communion liturgy, representing the congregation, with the care seeker. Otherwise, a separate group may be formed to take on these communion responsibilities, and they would meet for one or two sessions and then as needed if issues arise that require ongoing conversation.

This care group might meet monthly as they develop their sense of mission and identity and then work on ground rules, boundaries, and ethics. Focus could then move to exploring the four narrative practices (attitude, presence, listening, and questioning), especially the first three. As they become comfortable with these foundational elements, they might shift to quarterly meetings, where they would continue to look at practical, pastoral, and spiritual topics, especially issues that relate specifically to the circumstances in which their care seekers find themselves. The learning process would be similar to the one for Parish Companions. Membership numbers would vary depending on the demographics of the congregation but would usually be between eight and twelve members plus the facilitator and/or consultant.

Care Groups for Hospitalizations and Related Needs

Another care group might be one that serves as a congregational link for people experiencing hospitalization from accidents, surgery, and illness for themselves or an immediate family member. This group would work with the pastoral staff and would be on call, usually serving one week every two or three months. Because hospitalizations are so much shorter in today's world, members of this care team might have to focus on visiting prior to planned hospitalizations and/or sending cards or making phone calls immediately after discharge. Some hospital situations (a cancer diagnosis or heart attack, for example) might lead to a referral for a Parish Companion relationship during the resultant lifestyle transition.

This group would also need significant training and support similar to the other teams that do one-on-one visitation. Generally, they would focus on the first set of materials (ground rules and identity for the group itself and ethics and boundaries in care relationships) and then the set of narrative practices, especially attitude, presence, and listening. A third area for focus during the first year of this group would be theology, spirituality, and the use of religious resources. Quite often, people who are in an immediate health crisis find great comfort in familiar religious resources and spiritually oriented conversation. This would be a particularly important consultation issue for care teams that work in the health care context.

These curricular topics and the process of group development would probably require monthly meetings for the first year and then quarterly support and continuing education meetings as the group members identify issues they would like to discuss further. The size of the group will depend on the size and situation of the congregation in order to minimize on-call frequency for the members.

Care Groups for Continuing Connections

There are care groups we would put under the category of "keeping connected." The group mentioned previously that emerged out of the pandemic shutdowns would be one such example. That group of thirty-five people contacted the whole congregation through monthly cards and calls to make sure people continued to feel connected and cared for during the pandemic. This particular care group had one session of consultation about making phone calls, listening carefully to things like tone of voice (since facial and body language clues weren't available), and understanding ethics and boundaries. Then they met as a group via video conferencing every couple of months for consultation on issues that arose during their visits and to give and receive support.

Other connection-type groups might be established to follow up with visitors or to befriend new members of the congregation. These groups would benefit from an orientation session as well as one focusing on issues like boundaries and attentive listening. The pastoral staff might like them to explore other topics as well. They would meet periodically for consultation about their work and for ongoing support and should be closely linked to the pastoral staff related to new members.

HANDS-ON CARE GROUPS

Many other kinds of care teams can be created for congregations in order to maximize both member participation and strong care networks for times of need. "Hands-on" groups might include teams that rake leaves or do simple repair projects for folks unable to take care of those kinds of needs on their own. A group might rotate responsibilities for driving a church bus to pick up congregants for worship. Groups might provide food for people in a short-term crisis or transition (a new baby, recovery from an illness, and the like) or run errands for a day for those kinds of situations.

These hands-on groups need the same kind of support and consultation that other teams need. They should meet for an orientation session that addresses boundaries, confidentiality, and clarity of mission and then meet periodically to talk about their work and process any concerns they might have. Because they might not meet as often as other groups, they should have a contact person (pastor or designated volunteer coordinator, for example) who is available for consultation when issues arise.

Hospitality Groups

Other care groups offer hospitality, although many of these groups are very hands-on as well. This might include a knitting group that makes prayer shawls or a funeral hospitality group that provides a meal after funerals and memorial services. Prayer groups might fit in this category. The important thing with groups like these and those in the prior category is that they are understood to be part of the care team network and supported accordingly, including installation as a care team. They should be invited to gather for support and to identify their ministry goals. They should develop guidelines and ground rules to maximize their work as well as their connections to one another. They should engage in conversation with a facilitator or consultant about boundaries and confidentiality as well as topics particularly appropriate to their area of ministry (for example, grief dynamics for the funeral team). And they should meet periodically (maybe once a year) with a representative from the congregational staff or leadership team that invites conversation and support and offers appreciation.

There are few limits to the kinds of care groups that can be developed to meet the needs of congregations. As you can see from this listing, the key aspects to creating and supporting any care group in the church are acknowledgment within the congregation; appropriate conversations about boundaries, confidentiality, presence, and careful listening;

and regular meetings for support and consultation about issues pertinent to the ministry of each group. Also crucial to all of these groups is congregational awareness and buy-in of their ministries. They should be commissioned annually in a worship service, and there should be regular communication about their mission and practices to the congregation through newsletters, announcements, and administrative reports. They should be seen as engaged, inclusive, and essential to the life of the congregation.

In the next chapter, we will discuss in more detail some of the strategies needed to create a pastoral care network in the congregation.

A QUESTION TO CONSIDER: What does generating a dynamic, multilayered program of pastoral care mean for a church, and what kinds of care groups would be most valuable in your congregation?

6

Developing Networks of Care

Three assertions have been operative throughout this book. First, we believe that increased attentiveness to the practices of care can foster a deeper and more profound experience of connection in congregations. Such attitudes and postures, in turn, nurture congregational formation and enhance the well-being of the community. Second, we are committed to training laypeople to participate in the ministries of care because as they become better at offering care to one another, they also strengthen their spiritual and relational well-being. Third, this training model is built around values and structures that are possible in any congregation. It is to this last point that we now turn as we reflect on some practical steps in developing networks of care within a congregation.

Communities of any size can participate in the model of care articulated in this book. Knowing that every congregation is unique makes it impossible to provide a universal template that works for all contexts and settings. The starting point in any church is to discern where more formalized structures are warranted. Asking a series of questions and identifying some common responses and themes can assist a community as they imagine ways to move forward. Some congregations may want to develop networks such as those described in chapter 5, while others may start with something smaller, such as a hands-on group or visitation group.

Exploring and Listening

The initial step in developing a network of care is to identify a small cadre of people who can function as an advisory task force. While some congregations may already have a care committee that responds to needs and crises as they arise, the role of this group is slightly different. The task force has four functions: naming current, formal, and informal care networks in the congregation; identifying the diverse needs of the congregation; imagining possibilities for ministry; and developing strategies for moving forward. Each of these activities needs to be done collaboratively as the group invites conversation, listens deeply and broadly, and negotiates among the many needs and ideas. Ultimately, members of this group may choose to continue as networks of care are developed, evaluated annually, and reimagined for the future. Alternatively, a new committee may be formed to carry out this function.

At every step, the task force invites broad participation across the congregation, recognizing that while not everyone in the congregation will be involved in the formal structures that are created, involving more people in early conversations will create a stronger sense that the ministry of care is connected to the congregation's overall mission. The invitations for these conversations should be just that: invitational, with an understanding that those in dialogue with the committee are offering ideas and insights rather than necessarily becoming care companions. This approach leads to a stronger buy-in among congregational members because more voices and ideas are engaged in the process.

Identifying Current Structures of Care

The first function of the task force is to identify current informal and formal care networks in the congregation. The goal of this step is not to assess whether these ministries are effective or good; rather, the goal is to appreciate that care is already part of the everyday ministry of a congregation. These informal structures are to be affirmed as signs of a caring congregation.

Conversations with staff (ordained and lay), committees, and other small groups can assist in the gathering of information. How are the activities of care currently embodied in the congregation? Are the caring activities of the congregation perceived to be the responsibility of the pastoral staff? What church school classes or small groups within the congregation may already be offering care in diverse and informal ways? Exploring current practices captures and affirms a fuller picture of what is already being done in the congregation.

Likewise, reflecting on times in an individual's or family's life when care is most needed can point toward some of the ways the church is already involved with one another as well as identify where additional care might be needed. Who is helping people think about what it means to be a parent or about how to nurture the spiritual journey of teens and young adults? Who works with people who are formalizing their commitments to one another through marriage or covenant services? Who supports those who have lost jobs or who have moved from one place to another? What church school class or informal group reaches out to those who have aging parents or who are aging themselves? Where do people with mental health concerns find support in their spiritual journey? Who is tending to people who are losing a loved one or grieving a recent loss? Task force members might be surprised to discover how much good ministry is already being done in their congregation.

Naming how everyday care is currently being addressed within a congregation has two benefits. First, since many congregations have informal structures such as church school classes, age-defined groups, or other gatherings that are already offering care, identifying them affirms what people are already doing as part of the community of faith. Since care is fundamental to the values we espouse as Christians, it is important to acknowledge those who are actively caring for others. Second, it is possible in this process to identify how training in narrative care among the congregation's current care companions might support their work.

Identifying and Prioritizing Needs

A second function of the advisory task force is to identify and prioritize the needs of a congregation. One of the reasons it is not possible to provide a universal model for care in every congregation is that every community has a unique set of needs. In addition, a church's context makes a difference in what resources are available outside the congregation. Rural areas, for example, may lack resources to address mental and/or physical health issues, while areas where people move frequently may lack opportunities for small groups to form and endure. Similarly, while common issues such as grief or loss, family life, or tending to mental health are part of every congregation, more urgent local needs might be identified to provide a focus for a ministry team.

Imagining Possibilities

The third job of the advisory task force is to imagine potential strategies for responding to the needs that have been named. As we have noted, care networks ought to be informed by dialogue with congregational members and not be developed by a few people on a committee or by the pastoral staff. Identifying possible responses to needs requires imagination as well as deep listening. Not every idea will be feasible, but every idea ought to be heard. If this stage of the work is done collaboratively, it will support a mutual investment in the ministry of care throughout the congregation.

A reminder here is important: the church cannot meet every care need through a formal structure or network. Hence this advisory group should not only think about what groups within the congregation might be helpful to initiate but also wonder about other community groups or agencies that might partner with the congregation in addressing needs. Other congregations in the area or region may also become partners, such as coordinating efforts and resources for responding to grief or loss.

Developing Responses

Most congregations cannot respond to all the needs in a congregation; instead, they must discern which ones are most vital to them at any season in the community's life. Without a doubt, however, more ideas about how to support people through a caring network will be generated than will be possible to implement in any congregation. As the advisory task force does their work, they might consider starting with a smaller initiative. This will give time for people to learn about the network of care groups, to discern how to participate in them, to develop some patterns for training, and to evaluate the effectiveness of the ministry. The spectrum of care in a congregation can be vast, and it is helpful for churches to faithfully discern what is possible, given the need for leaders, ministry team members, financial commitments, time, and more. The goal of this planning is to imagine where more structured training and implementation might be feasible.

As the task force begins to identify potential groups, they also need to give thought to assessing the congregation's willingness to participate as care seekers as well as volunteers who become care companions. This strategizing also assists a church in gaining clarity about how the specific activities of care fit into the larger vision of the church. Each care team needs to understand they have a place in the larger mission of the congregation.

Organizing (Leadership and Accountability)

For the care network to have vitality and clarity, it is important that issues of leadership and accountability for the work be addressed. This attention to structure reinforces the notion that care occurs through a network of responses and not simply through the work of individual congregational members or autonomous groups. The structure enhances the ability of these groups to work together, providing lines of accountability and communication.

The Role of Pastoral Leaders

Conversations in the task force lead to mutually agreed-upon lines of accountability and decisions about the scope of care for each ministry team. Most church polities, regardless of the size of the congregation, suggest that the pastoral staff or lead pastor has specific responsibility for pastoral care. Their role in establishing a network of care is significant. Not only must the pastoral staff buy into the possibilities that are imagined by the task force, but they also must bear responsibility for the lines of communication within the whole church. Establishing ministry teams is not dependent on having a large church or a large staff; rather, the point here is that the identified pastoral leader, often alongside a governing board or committee, carries the responsibility and authority to offer care on behalf of a congregation.

It is a mistake for those in pastoral leadership to assume that training laypersons in the ministry of care relieves them of responsibility for pastoral care or that care teams are developed primarily to "assist" the pastor. Training congregants to care for one another does not take away the pastor's ongoing responsibilities for such things as identifying and assessing more complex pastoral needs and making appropriate referrals. The pastoral staff, regardless of its size, needs to be familiar with the care program at every level both for purposes of referring people to the care ministries and for overseeing the program itself. The coordinator of the care network reports to the pastor as they oversee the day-to-day work of the program. The pastoral leader plays a role in keeping the work of care in front of the church, providing transparency by noting its value to the congregation and the oversight they provide. Communication to the congregation about the work of the task force, the development of care teams, opportunities for training, and invitations to specific people to participate in the care ministries of the church are all part of the pastor's continuing role. Announcements in bulletins or newsletters, appropriate illustrations in sermons about the gift of mutual care, and opportunities to formally commission or identify those who are functioning in the care ministries of a congregation can be significant in keeping the church informed and involved.

The governing board or formal leadership of the church also carries a significant role in affirming the work of the care ministry. Not only do they support the efforts outlined above, but they are also charged with thinking through any logistical matters related to the ministry. Someone will want to explore, for example, whether additional insurance is needed for a congregation, since the laypersons involved in the caring ministries act as representatives of the congregation and are accountable to them. And as is true with every volunteer in the church, the appropriate procedures for background checks should be followed.

THE ROLE OF THE COORDINATOR

A coordinator for the ministry needs to be identified early in the process. This person may be part of the staff or even the lead pastor. In some congregations, an associate pastor or a parish nurse might take on this role. The coordinator need not be an expert in counseling, but they should have the personality and background that allows them to see the congregational care needs in a healthy and decentered way. They also need to be able to encourage collaborative leadership within the groups. The coordinator carries the major responsibility for tending to the care networks. They are charged with helping clarify the structures of the ministry as well as keeping the networks connected to the larger vision of the church.

Alongside the lead pastor and other staff persons, the coordinator keeps the work of the caring ministry before the congregation, receives referrals from colleagues and church members, and identifies people in the congregation who are experiencing needs. This person matches those in need with those who are trained to offer care, maintains records, and follows up as needed with other pastoral staff or with referral agencies. In addition, they are responsible for identifying and recruiting those who will be part of the care team's training program.

Care Network Members

Pastoral care builds on meaningful and thoughtful conversations, and the process of recruiting participants to be care companions requires the same. The coordinator spends time talking with people who are interested in serving on a care team and discerns with them what kind of ministry best suits their gifts and graces. Two realities exist side by side when recruiting people to participate in the training for care ministries. On the one hand, because care belongs to the entire congregation, everyone ought to be able to find a place to participate in the formal and informal caregiving network. On the other hand, people sometimes need support as they discern the most appropriate place for their service. Not everyone who wants to participate as a care companion may have the right combination of gifts or time available to do so. One of the keys to developing healthy ministries is to find ways for the coordinator and potential group member to mutually discern where best to serve.

Honest conversation between the coordinator and a potential member of the care team is essential in the recruitment process. The coordinator's work is not simply to assign people to situations or those in need of care; rather, they invite people to reflect on where they might best serve the community. Some congregations may decide that it is better to offer invitations to those whom they perceive to be well suited for the more long-term work of care companions as described in chapter 5 rather than depend upon a voluntary network. For other care teams, a congregation might decide to have a more flexible point of entry for volunteers that allows them to choose how they wish to participate. Helping people discern the right training program to be involved in can enhance the overall ministry of the congregation. Conversations about the nature of the care that is being offered can help people discern whether they would be more comfortable in a telephone ministry that reaches out to those living alone or would want to become a care companion who journeys with someone in long-term situations such as through illness, death, or grief. The same person may be adept at both but, because of life situations, may need to choose one over the other. Mutuality supports the agency of individuals to make careful choices about how best to engage in ministry.

When identifying persons who might become part of the care network, several qualities are important. First, care companions should be seen as trustworthy by others. Because respecting and maintaining confidentiality is a cornerstone of good pastoral care and care companions often work with people who are in vulnerable situations, the congregation must be confident that they will not talk about care seekers to other people or share stories of their visits with others.

Second, those who participate in the ministry of care need to engage in significant training to develop their capacities for narrative care prior to being assigned as a care companion. It is important to recruit people who are open to learning with others, who are willing to seek and offer consultation with one another, and who want to learn in collaborative ways.

Third, programs need to recruit people who are open-minded and ready to explore new ideas. They need to be committed to an invitational and empowering posture in their offering of care. The narratives we invite and the way we support the storytelling of others are integral to listening and care. For care companions, this means we are open to whatever others wish to share and to setting aside our expectations of what conversations should look like. The goal is to empower others along their journey.

Fourth, although care companions often receive a great deal of affirmation for and good feelings from their presence with others, it's important they do not turn to care ministries in order to get their emotional or friendship needs met. Mutual care acknowledges that we connect to one another in ways that are significant. We are touched when people listen to us deeply, just as we are often moved when we have the honor of hearing someone else's sacred stories. There is mutuality in this process. Being part of a care team also presents an opportunity to develop friends and peers within the network as well as deepen relationships within the congregation. But care companions must acknowledge the difference between being a care companion and a close friend.

Finally, care companions are open to being changed by their experiences. People who are open to learning about themselves and about care are surprised by the impact of how being a care companion makes a difference in their own lives. While it is not appropriate to enter the work of care with the sole purpose of growing, it is also impossible to participate in the learning communities without experiencing an increase in self-awareness and a change in one's perspectives. And as a result, care companions usually experience a ripple effect in other areas of their lives as they alter the ways that they are present with others.

Training and Collaborative Learning

While there are many ways to provide training for the ministry teams, we want to offer a few suggestions. It is critical that the groups meet regularly for teaching, learning, support, community building, and mutual guidance. These meetings are intended to support those who are engaged in the work by enhancing skills of attitude, presence, listening, and questioning. One of the more significant tasks of the coordinator is to keep the groups focused on training rather than just becoming a place of personal support for issues that, while important, are not part of the work of caring with others.

A common mistake new caregivers make is to imagine that we need to know a lot about counseling or psychological theory. Instead, what is most needed is someone who can help the care companions imagine their way into narrative care—listening deeply and thoughtfully, asking meaningful questions, and maintaining a narrative lens. Since it is a more consultative approach, the narrative model does not require the same kind of supervision as we often think about in counseling models. Both of us have written about supervision from the perspectives of narrative (Christie) and collaborative (Joretta) theory. We understand the importance of education, teaching, and learning and the role of supervision. The narrative perspective, however, relies more on a collaborative model among peers who are doing the work of pastoral care with members of the congregation.

Churches in cities or larger towns might be able to find a narrative counselor in the area who can support the training program. However, most churches will have difficulty finding someone with narrative expertise. This does not mean that a congregation can't engage in narrative care. The narrative practices identified in this book, along with the ideas offered about collaborative learning, can facilitate the work of the training program. It is important that anyone invited in as a resource see themselves not as the "expert" in the room but as a cocollaborator around the generative activity of communal learning. Ultimately, group members will learn to rely on one another as they encourage narrative practices. Together, they work to stay focused on the stories of others, to ask beautiful questions, to invite stories of resiliency and hope, and to support one another in the task of theological reflection.

Narrative care is not an interventionist model where assessment and advice are the goals; rather, it builds on mutual collaboration and conversation. In a parallel way, training groups recognize that their best learning takes place in conversation with one another. As the networks focus on the building of their narrative skills, they also experience care with one another and can imagine more freely what it means to offer good narrative care. The group meetings can help people wonder with one another about a particular situation that someone has encountered or role-play how to ask questions that invite diverse stories. The purpose of these groups is not to create minicounselors but to assist one another in becoming more adept at inviting stories that have the potential for transformation and witnessing stories that are life giving and hope filled. Training can also include reflection on books or articles related to topics of interest, theological discussions about themes that emerge in the practices of care, or role play that helps demonstrate and explore new ways of being a companion to others.

People in the congregation or the community who have experienced good supportive care might join a meeting, as they can attest to the importance of deep listening and the power of good questions. Because theological reflection is central to care in the context of a congregation, a training coordinator can also seek people who can help them think theologically. Chaplains, for example, can be partners in collaborative learning. Or other pastoral leaders—including ecumenical and interfaith partners, who bring an expertise in narrative care—can participate from a distance or in person.

Ongoing Evaluation and Redesign

The program we are describing in this book is organic and fluid with ebbs and flows that contribute to the overall work of care. We are not offering a specific set of lessons or a fixed template for training. This program grows out of the needs of a congregation and the gifts and graces of its members. Thus, the leaders of the program—pastoral staff and laypersons—need to reflect at least annually with care teams on what is working well in the networks of care, what might be changed, what new needs of the congregation are emerging, and whether some ministries can be ended. These conversations offer opportunities to reshape programs in ways that make them more vital.

Assessment might occur at two levels. First, it is important to ask how a particular group is functioning. What do the individuals in the group experience? How is their spiritual and relational life changing as a result of participating in the groups? Are there things that need to be addressed by leaders and group members to help the group function in a healthier way?

Second, leaders also reflect on how the overall ministry of care is functioning in the congregation. Are people aware of and responding to the invitation to companion with one another either to address specific needs or to offer care? Are some ministries no longer needed or could the work be done through a more informal network? Could a particular ministry join with a group outside the congregation to address needs in the larger community? Have new needs been identified to which the church might respond? Honest reflection on what is happening both within care groups and on behalf of the entire church can ensure a care ministry's vitality.

Toward a More Compassionate Church

We wrote this book because we believe a narrative lens in lay pastoral care makes a positive difference in the lives of individuals, families, and the congregation. By inviting stories that contribute to resiliency and hope and offer witness to people sharing their experiences, a narrative approach to pastoral care changes not only the individuals but the community itself. As people feel more cared for, they also experience a deeper connection to the community and to the transformative power of God. As a result, there is a deeper vitality in the congregation and among those who participate in the care programs. As people learn with one another and care with one another, connections become deeper, and spiritual growth becomes a bigger part of the web of congregational life.

Because theological reflection is central to the work of pastoral care, the collaborative groups involved in the training of care companions offer multiple opportunities for people to think together about God's power and limitations, the role and meaning of suffering, and the importance of community as an embodiment of God's care. Together, these groups deepen the theological discourse in a congregation as they invite others to reflect on the values and commitments that shape their theology. The congregation, by engaging in these ministries, will develop a deeper sense of vision and mission as they participate in care and become a more compassionate community. Together, they witness the way that God lives and moves in their corporate and individual lives. This transformation is described in the words of a staff person who coordinates pastoral care in one congregation:

> Through the growth and strength of our care ministry programs, I have witnessed transformation within our church community. Care team members connect with fellow congregants and, through their careful listening, invite the story that needs to be shared. And these connections, holding these stories, are holy. Always. I remember a visit with a woman in our congregation, and she shared this: "You know, all my life, I have felt like I have been on the outside, but at church, I feel like I am on the inside." My heart was full of gratitude for this powerful witness to what it looks like to be welcomed and loved. A strong care ministry program is an essential pillar on which a church community is built, for it lays the foundation for holy connections and sacred storytelling that are empowering and a blessing for all.

People have rich and sometimes complicated lives. They deserve the best of care from laypersons and ordained clergy. This book stands on a commitment to a narrative lens in developing pastoral care ministries in congregations of any size or context. In the preface, we shared the convictions that compelled us to spend time writing about a new model of care that values narrative companions who take time to listen to our stories and who invite us to craft visions for our lives. Our experiences in the church and in the seminary—with pastors, students, and parishioners—lead us to believe that a narrative lens on pastoral care can make a significant difference in the lives of those with whom we journey. The attitudes we bring to care—the way we communicate presence, our ability to listen carefully and deeply, the curiosities we carry, and the questions we ask—all contribute to the power of a narrative approach.

We hope that you embrace the deep values we have tried to communicate about narrative and collaborative care. We believe that this model not only serves individuals, families, and communities who are experiencing a particular need but can also alter the lives of those involved in the care networks. Ultimately, the work transforms the life of a congregation as it deepens its ability to care at a fundamental level and invites people into life-changing possibilities.

A QUESTION TO CONSIDER: As you think about developing or enhancing a congregational lay caregiving network in your setting, what are the main ideas from this book that you would like to implement, and how might you assess whether your church is becoming a more compassionate community?

Appendixes

Our focus in these appendixes is on providing some practical resources for coordinators to use as they develop lay care team networks for their congregations. As we have said throughout this book, we are not wanting in any way to be prescriptive in our descriptions of various care groups with whom we have worked. Yet we think that some suggestions and examples of group resources might be helpful. We have concluded these appendixes with a set of brief stories written by members of a current lay care group from a local congregation. We hope you find these resources helpful in your work.

Christie Neuger and Joretta Marshall

Appendix Contents

Appendix A

Resources for Forming Care Groups

Policies and Procedures for Care Groups

The following policies and procedures were developed for different kinds of care groups, including a companion group, a hospital visitation group, and a food preparation and delivery group. These documents served three purposes. They were used in the recruitment process so all volunteers would know what was expected of them. They were used for communication with the congregation so the church would get a good sense of the care groups' purposes. And they were used for administration so those coordinating and overseeing these programs would be clear about the nature and scope of the group being defined and so that clarity would be sustained during leadership transitions.

Parish Companions

Definitions, Policies, and Procedures

What is the parish companion program?

The parish companion program of _ Church matches people who wish to receive visits from a pastoral care companion during a time of significant transition with members of the congregation who have volunteered for and been trained in pastoral care visitation. The program is under the oversight of a coordinator, who will call upon resources such as trainers, presenters, mentors, and the like as needed in consultation with the pastor. In addition, a leadership team includes the coordinator, the pastor, and potentially, a trainer/consultant for the group.

What are the goals of the parish companion program?

- To better meet the extended pastoral care needs of congregants experiencing significant transitions in their lives
- To better create a dynamic community of care within the church
- To offer training and supervision to parish members who serve in this program, enhancing their lives and the communities in which they participate
- To create collaborative partnerships for pastoral care among clergy, parish nurses, and congregants who participate in the program

Who serves as a parish companion?

Congregational members are invited to participate in this program. Those invitations will be based on the leadership team's assessment of potential participants who seem best suited for this kind of work, who currently have the time to follow through with the care relationship and with the ongoing training, and who have indicated an interest in this kind of ministry. The potential participant will be invited to an interview with the coordinator and/or their consultants where interest, suitability, and the parameters of the program will be discussed. Mutual decision-making about joining the program will emerge from the discussion.

The qualities most needed in a parish companion include the following:

- good boundaries
- ability to put one's own needs and inclinations aside during a visit
- good listening skills
- ability to put aside the need to "fix" or "problem-solve"
- compassionate heart
- nonjudgmental attitude
- strong sense of self
- team orientation
- commitment to ongoing training and consultation
- ability to follow through with a long-term commitment (normally, six months to a year)

Who receives care through this program?

The program is designed primarily for people who are experiencing a significant life transition and who might be helped by a supportive, caring pastoral relationship. Transitions might include the recent death of a loved one, a devastating medical diagnosis, a significant relationship breakup, a move to a care facility, a family crisis, a job loss, or becoming a primary caregiver to a chronically ill family member. These are examples of potential care receiver situations but are not exhaustive of the possibilities. Situations that would most likely not be eligible for this program would include people with significant mental illness, minor children, and others whom the coordinator or pastor believes have needs greater than a parish companion can address. The care receivers are assessed by the coordinator and/or the pastor to see if they would be open to and would likely benefit from regular visits by a trained parish companion for no more than one year. They are matched with a parish companion who seems most likely to be helpful in this particular relationship.

The coordinator will fully explain the nature of the parish companion program to a potential care receiver, including time and boundary limits as well as the parameters of confidentiality, before making a match with a parish companion.

Family members or close friends might also recommend a person who is not a member of the congregation to receive care in this program. Their eligibility for the program would depend on the availability of a parish companion and the closeness of their relationship to the congregation, as determined by the coordinator and pastor.

What training do parish companions receive before they begin a care relationship with a congregant?

A parish companion receives initial training in the following:

- self-assessment and self-awareness
- defining an appropriate care relationship
- ethics and boundaries
- active listening
- the use of questions in pastoral care
- how to begin a parish companion relationship
- the use of religious resources in a parish companion relationship

Following completion of this initial curriculum, a parish companion relationship may be initiated. However, monthly training and consultation continue, addressing topics such as the following:

- the dynamics of grief
- the dynamics of a crisis
- the differences between grief and depression

- caregiving in the aftermath of an end-of-life diagnosis
- caregiving through issues of aging
- caregiving through issues of relationship dissolution
- knowing when to ask for consultation/supervision
- ending the care relationship

These monthly training sessions also include a group discussion of the particular caregiving relationships of the participants, done sensitively and with confidentiality.

What are the general policies and guidelines for the parish companion program?

- The primary role of a parish companion is that of a compassionate listener and a supportive presence. The parish minister does not provide for physical needs, such as transportation or chores. If a request for these kinds of services arises, the parish companion refers the request to the coordinator.
- Parish companions maintain confidentiality about whom they are visiting and all conversations they have. The parish companion may discuss situations and address questions and concerns with the coordinator, pastor, or lead consultant in a confidential setting. In the group consultations, the focus will be on issues that parish companions experience rather than on the details of the care receivers.
- Parish companion visits are limited to a reasonable amount of time (typically an hour or less, unless there is an unusual need). Visits occur at least once a month and probably more often at the beginning of the relationship.
- A parish companion relationship extends no longer than one year.

- Active parish companions keep in close contact with the coordinator about the status of their visits and participate in monthly group training and consultation sessions. (Parish companions without an active care-giving relationship are encouraged to attend the monthly sessions.)
- Parish companions do not accept gifts from their care receivers or engage in any activities that reflect their own needs rather than those of the care receivers.
- Parish companions may negotiate when and where they meet with their care receivers as long as those meeting places and times are deemed appropriate by the coordinator. If in doubt, companions discuss their situation with the coordinator or in a group consultation.
- Parish companions do not respond to emergencies, such as late-night calls, spontaneous needs for an immediate visit, and so forth. If crises arise, these are referred to the pastor or the parish nurse.
- If the parish companion has any concerns about the health and well-being of the care receiver, they should immediately contact the pastor or the coordinator for consultation.

Parish Ministers

Mission

Parish ministers seek to reach out as representatives of the congregation to those who are in a crisis or have a short-term need of care. This usually includes hospital visits or requested visits to a person living in a long-term or transitional care facility. Knowing there is a role for both pastor and lay in a crisis situation, parish ministers are an extended ministry of the church and serve as tangible witnesses to the care of the community.

Procedures and Practices

- Parish ministers must make a commitment to be on call one week every three months.
- The program and communications coordinator will notify the parish minister of any hospitalizations or admissions to a care facility during the week they are on call. If possible, parish ministers should visit the member within twenty-four hours of being called.
- Parish ministers should do the following:
  - Demonstrate the love of God to those served.
  - Remember that listening is more important than talking.
  - As appropriate, pray for and with the person being visited.
  - Observe confidentiality at all times. Confidentiality means one does not ever name names or reveal situations unless permission is first granted by the care receiver or a person authorized to speak for them.
  - Take a prayer shawl to the person if they have not received one previously.
- After the visit, parish ministers report it to the coordinator for record keeping and follow-up. If there are issues or concerns, please share them with the coordinator at this time so they can engage the appropriate staff as necessary.
- Parish ministers attend the parish minister meeting every other month for conversation, support, and training.

- Parish ministers provide the coordinator with the information needed for background checks.
- Parish ministers attend the commissioning service for the caring ministry teams.

Soul Food

Soul Food: Meals for Times of Need is a ministry of hospitality and care of __ Church. It extends the congregation's care to those who would benefit by receiving meals in times of transition, disruption, or hardship, such as the birth of a child, the return from a hospitalization, a recovery from an illness, a death in the family, and the like. These meals are prepared and delivered by congregants to congregants, knowing that mutual acts of care are fundamental to the mission and purpose of our church.

Congregants who are anticipating or experiencing a need for the Soul Food ministry or congregants who know of someone in the church who might benefit from it are asked to contact the pastor or parish nurse. Congregants who wish to volunteer for this ministry, or who want to contribute to it in some other way, are asked to contact the parish nurse.

Leadership Team

Pastor:
Parish Nurse:
Coordinator/Consultant:

Procedures and Practices

When personal or family disruptions come to the attention of the church staff, the household will be contacted and asked if they would be interested in receiving up to three meals provided by members of the church. If they wish to receive this service, they will be asked to fill out a preference form identifying the specifics of their need (including any food allergies or limitations). The Soul Food team that is on call for that period will coordinate food preparation and delivery.

Soul Food volunteers are arranged by teams (usually four members to a team) that are on call for a specific month. When a need arises, the volunteer coordinators alert the team to the situation and give them pertinent information.

For times when there is more demand for meals than is expected in a month, a small supply of frozen meals will be kept at the church to be delivered to families in times of need.

VOLUNTEERS ARE ASKED TO DO THE FOLLOWING:

- Go through an initial orientation process, including a background check.
- Sign up to be on call for one or two months during the year or to serve as an occasional backup volunteer.
- Along with that month's other team members, prepare or provide up to three full meals for the household and deliver them during the time windows designated by the recipients.
- Prepare a simple, well-balanced meal. Examples of nutritious meals include homemade soups and casseroles, pot roast or roasted chicken with potatoes and vegetables, salad in a bag, and hot or cold pasta entrées. Takeout food from a restaurant or deli is also appropriate. Dessert is optional.
- Maintain food at safe temperatures from preparation to delivery. Include directions for preparing the meal if needed. Identify foods that need to be kept refrigerated or that may be reheated or frozen for later use.

- Deliver the food to the household but not stay to visit with household members.
- Maintain confidentiality by not sharing food recipients' names or situations with anyone.
- Report any problems or concerns to the coordinator as soon as possible.

Program coordinator(s) are asked to do the following:

- Receive a notification from the pastor or the parish nurse that there is a Soul Food need.
- Contact the household to discern the nature of the food need and arrange for them to fill out the preference form (either over the phone or in person).
- Contact the on-call Soul Food team and alert them to the need for meals, inviting them to arrange food preparation/provision and delivery among themselves.
- Follow up with the team to make sure all has gone smoothly. Report any problems or concerns to the pastor or parish nurse.
- Maintain a current list of the monthly on-call teams and notify the parish nurse if additional volunteers are needed.

Learning Community Ground Rules

We believe all groups and committees in congregations should generate their own ground rules for how they will function together to best carry out their mission so they have full ownership of them. They create these ground rules by simply asking the question, "How do we best work together in safe and effective ways?" Ground rules specify the communal expectations, enable members to hold themselves and one another accountable, and head off potential conflicts within the group. Ground rules can take a variety of forms, but they should be as specific as possible, especially about topics like confidentiality and participation expectations.

PARISH COMPANIONS

Ground Rules

1. We will try to arrive at and leave group meetings on time.
2. We will practice confidentiality.
   - We will change or disguise names and other identifying information when we consult about visits.
   - We will not divulge any experiences shared in the group with others, even in our own families.
   - We may share things that we have learned from the group but without naming anyone else's experience.
   - We will not let anyone in the congregation know the name of someone we are visiting.
   - We will not acknowledge that we are visiting someone, even if they seem to be aware we are visiting a person they know.
   - We will not initiate a care conversation with someone we are visiting if we are in church or any other public place.
3. We will engage in respectful listening with one another.
   - We will not interrupt or hold side conversations when we are in a group conversation.
   - We will turn off our cell phones before group begins.

- We will take responsibility for our own participation in the group while making room for all group members to participate.

4. We will ask opening-up questions and engage in reflective listening in our visit consultations rather than giving advice to one another.
5. We will invite joy and humor into our group process.
6. We will acknowledge that these ground rules are dynamic, and we will review them periodically.

Care Ministers

Ground Rules

1. Confidentiality: We will practice confidentiality, meaning we do not share with people outside of the group anything from our visits or consultations about them. We will not talk about other group members' experiences or stories shared in the group.
2. Respect: We agree to consciously respect one another's belief and value systems and act consistently with that respect. We especially will be respectful of differences and attempt to learn from our differences and disagreements.
3. Feedback: We will prioritize asking questions rather than giving advice or sharing our own ideas about ways to offer care. We will try to be direct, respectful, and kind in our case consultations.
4. Sharing time in group: We will be aware of our own patterns of communication and monitor those individually and collectively so we have conversational fairness in the group.

5. Review: We agree to review and revise these ground rules as needed.

Forms Used in Care Ministries

When starting up care teams, standardized forms allow for clear communication and oversight. The first form provides information about a potential companion / care seeker relationship and is completed by the pastor or coordinator of the program. The second is a record-keeping form used by the care companion to keep track of care visits. The third form is to be used to record the end of a care relationship.

Care Companion Referral

Confidential

Name ____

Address ____

Phone ______________________ Cell phone _________________

Email address ____

Age _______________________ Gender pronouns ____________

Occupation __________________ Work phone _______________

Best time to contact ___________________________________

Best way to contact ___________________________________

Others in the home ____________________________________

Reason for companion request/invitation?

____

____

____

Any other information the care seeker wishes to have shared?

____

____

____

Emergency contact information:

Name ____

Relationship ____

Address ____

Phone numbers: home _______________ cell _________________

work _______________

Has the care seeker been informed about the Parish Companion program, especially issues of confidentiality, consultation, time frames, and the role of the parish companion? Explain.

Has the care seeker consented to being a participant in this program?

Yes ______ No ______

Form completed by __________________________ Date __________

Parish companion assigned ____________________ Date __________

Parish Companion Record of Visits

Confidential

Parish companion name ______________________________

Care seeker initials ______________________________

Date of first visit ______________ Length of visit ______________

Initiated by ______

Notes from visit

____

____

Visit # ______

Date of first visit ______________ Length of visit ______________

Initiated by ______

Notes from visit

____

____

Visit # ______

Date of first visit ______________ Length of visit ______________

Initiated by ______

Notes from visit

____

____

Visit # ______

Date of first visit ______________ Length of visit ______________

Initiated by ______

Notes from visit

____

____

Ending a Care Relationship

Confidential

Date:

1. Name of care companion ________________________
2. Name of care seeker ________________________
3. Date of initial contact ________________________
4. Date of last visit ________________________
5. Total number of visits ________________________
6. Reasons for initiating the companion relationship ____________
7. Reasons for ending the relationship (circle one)
   a. Completed as agreed by both
   b. Completed as designated by one of you
   c. Referred to another care provider
   d. Other reasons

____

____

____

____

8. Any follow-up or continuing relationship planned? If so, describe.

____

____

____

____

* *Adapted from Stephen Ministry Wrap-Up Form*

Appendix B

Resources for Care Companion Learning Groups

The following resources are designed to help the teaching and learning processes in lay care groups. We seek to be suggestive with these ideas and, through them, to encourage your own imagination about how to best learn together. The first section contains ideas for skill practices, especially for gaining competency in effective narrative listening and questioning. They are dependent on not only the role play practices but also the discussion and feedback that follow the exercises. The second section is on consultation methods so groups can reflect together on their visits. Again, feedback, discussion, and reflection are most important.

Skill Practice Exercises

Role Play Methods and Vignettes

In the group context, the coordinator takes on the care seeker role in the vignette, starting the conversation with a group member who plays the care companion role. The care seeker shares their story while the care companion offers narrative listening responses. The conversation continues for five to ten minutes while the rest of the group observes. At the end of that time, both the care seeker and the care companion evaluate their experience in the role play. Then the other group members offer their observations for general group discussion.

The tone is one of encouragement for the role play duo, and the focus is on a general exploration of best practices. After a few minutes of discussion, the coordinator and a new participant may begin a role play with a different vignette.

A variation of this exercise is also helpful. In this form, the coordinator plays the role of care seeker in a vignette, allowing all the group members, in rotation, to demonstrate reflective or narrative listening. The role play ends after each group member has rotated through the role of care companion twice. Then general discussion about how people felt about their experience in the role play takes place.

These exercises, which utilize a whole group model of participation, avoid the risks of just pairing group members with one another to practice on their own. All of the group members are able to listen to one another's reflective responses, thus enriching feedback and learning in the practice process.

Vignettes

a. A care seeker plans to revise their will after their spouse has died, wanting to be fair to all four children but knowing that one has greater needs and one has no need for financial help. The care seeker hopes to talk through what fairness means in this situation.
b. A care seeker has lost a best friend but doesn't feel there is much social support for this kind of grief. Yet this friend was very important to the care seeker, who explains, "No one else has ever mattered so much in my life, and I feel so alone." They don't know what to do to process these feelings.
c. A care seeker has an aging parent who has been diagnosed with Alzheimer's but who refuses to accept the diagnosis. The adult child doesn't know how to plan

for the future and support their parent (or deal with their own feelings).

d. A care seeker has been offered a promotion at work, but the new position will put them in a supervisory role over people who have been peers. They aren't sure whether to take the promotion or not.

e. A care seeker is trying to downsize in preparation for moving to a seniors' facility but is discovering they have emotional attachments to the many items they have collected or saved over the years.

Other Methods

A group member identifies an aspect of a situation with their care seeker about which they feel stuck or concerned. The group member raises the concern during the case consultation time (see "Case Consultation Methods," page 168) and asks for help exploring ways to best respond to the care seeker's situation. The facilitator may invite the group member to role-play the situation with another group member playing the care seeker. Or and often more helpfully, the care companion who has raised the concerns is asked whether they would like to play the part of their care seeker with another group member playing the care companion's role. The role play begins with the care companion's concern, and the conversation continues for five to ten minutes. The rest of the group observes.

At the end of the conversation, each role player shares how they experienced the conversation—what it felt to be the care seeker, any new insights either of them had, and so on. Then group members are invited to share their observations and questions. The companion who has raised the concern is invited to discuss how this role play has helped them consider possible ways to engage the troubling situation.

A variation on this exercise is for the group member who raises the concern to role-play the care seeker while the other group members rotate, each offering one potential narrative listening response or question at a time. This gives the concerned care companion a chance to see multiple potential ways to engage the care seeker at the point where they felt stuck. Discussion follows.

Case Consultation Methods

Consultation Method 1

So care companions can both learn about and maintain accountability for their ministry, each group meeting includes a time for participants who are currently in a care relationship to discuss their most recent visit(s). Generally, care companions share important aspects of the pastoral conversation and then ask for consultation on either the concerns they have about the care seeker's situation or, even more helpfully, some aspect of their own approach to care in this relationship. The care companion tries to be specific about their consultation request. For example, a group member may ask how to better move from a casual conversation to a more in-depth one or how to keep their own emotional reactions from taking over the conversation. Group members then invite reflection through comments and questions rather than giving advice. The group practices their care skills of attitude, presence, listening, and questioning in the group consultation process. The care companion is then asked to identify what she or he will be taking from the conversation back into their care relationship.

Consultation Method 2

A care companion in an active care relationship may decide to ask for consultation by sharing a brief *verbatim* (a written account, including—as best the writer can recall—who said what, body language and tone, and other relevant details) of the part of the visit about which they want feedback. This verbatim can be read by two group members so that the whole group can get a sense of how the conversation went. The presenting care companion may or may not participate in the reading, depending on whether they wish to get a new perspective on the conversation or instead present the tone of the conversation from their own memory.

After the verbatim reading, the care companion can identify their particular consultation focus to the group for discussion, or they may wish for the group to offer their perceptions without guidance from the companion. Again, the group members avoid advising or fixing and rely on their pastoral care skills. After the consultation, the coordinator may wish to ask the presenter and the group about how they experienced their discussion.

Appendix C

Boundaries: Resources for Group Presentation and Discussion

In this section, we move to various topics that may be appropriate for care groups as they seek to gain insights into and new perspectives of situations they will encounter in their visits. We expect some topics (boundaries and ethics, listening skills, grief care, and so on) to surface in care groups, and other topics may or may not surface, depending on the care visit contexts. The following are resources for facilitating useful discussions.

A Presentation Outline

I. Boundaries
   a. Types of boundaries include physical, emotional, time, space, gifts/favors/friendship, attitude, communications, access.
   b. Boundaries are internal, external, combination.
   c. Boundary discussions may start with the question, Where do I stop and others begin?
   d. Boundary claims include such things as the following:
      i. People have full ownership of their stories.
      ii. People are free to interpret their own experiences.
      iii. People are free to set their own priorities.
      iv. People don't have to feel the same way I do.
      v. People get to make their own decisions.

e. Possible problems in the care companion's boundaries include the following:
   i. *Touching others in uninvited, overly familiar, or unwelcome ways.*
   ii. *Wanting to give advice or direction to the care seeker.*
   iii. *Wanting to "do things" for the care seeker.*
   iv. *Wanting to make or carry out decisions for the care seeker.*
   v. *Feeling critical of the care seeker's lifestyle.*
   vi. *Using the care relationship to meet one's own needs.*
   vii. *Not maintaining confidentiality.*
f. Possible problems coming from difficulties with the care seeker's boundaries include the following:
   i. *Experiencing manipulation in the care relationship.*
   ii. *Getting calls or visits at inappropriate times or frequency.*
   iii. *Feeling guilty for not doing "enough."*
   iv. *Feeling that you should give or lend something.*
   v. *Feeling like you have to keep a secret from the care coordinator.*
g. People in all relationships experience boundary negotiations, but they get more complicated in lay care situations because (1) the care seeker is vulnerable and (2) roles shift from being fellow congregants to being in a care relationship.

II. Other ethical issues
   a. Maintaining confidentiality is key in caregiving ministries and needs to be meticulous.
   b. Staying within your care companion role and competencies is important.
      i. *Role clarity between a care companion and care seeker can be complex because of previous and current congregational participation. When in doubt about how to keep*

the care companion role primary in making visits, consult with the coordinator or with the care group.

ii. *If you are in doubt about what you are experiencing in the care relationship or what you are being asked to know or to do in that relationship, immediately seek consultation with the coordinator or pastor.*

c. Caregivers need to seek group and individual consultation regularly while in an active care relationship.

Discussion Question

Which boundary types might be the most challenging for you to maintain? Which are the easiest?

Vignettes for Role Play and Discussion

1. A parishioner comes up to a care companion and says, "I know that you visit with Jean from time to time. She told me that you are such a dear soul, but she wishes you would come earlier in the day and stay a bit longer. She also says that you don't always listen very well to her. I thought I should say something to you to help." The care receiver finds themselves angry, but they don't know if they are angry with Jean or the parishioner or themselves. They know they have been a bit impatient with Jean lately and rushed their visits and that they do get bored sometimes with her repeated stories. The care companion tells the parishioner that they think the visits are going just fine and that if Jean has complaints, she should tell her directly. Are there boundary issues?

2. A care minister has visited Jeff for several months, and they have good conversations. However, Jeff lately has been asking for a little extra help—nothing too extreme—like "Before you go, would you mind trying to fix my cable box? I seem to have it on the wrong channel or something" or "Would you mind picking up a few things at the grocery store for me before you come this week?" The care minister feels a bit uneasy with these requests, but they aren't big enough to worry about. However, the care minister begins to think about visiting less often or even asking the coordinator for a new care receiver. Are there boundary issues?

Appendix D

Rituals for Use in Care Relationships

If used carefully for special situations, rituals can be useful in pastoral care. In addition to using your own denominational or congregational liturgies for communion, we have included an alternative form that might be used in the care relationship. We also have included a ritual that might be used between a care companion and a care seeker as they bring their care relationship to a close.

Home Communion Visits

Part of lay pastoral care involves the use of religious resources. Home communion is one such resource. The benefits of doing home communion include (1) bringing the community of the church to a person who is unable to worship with a congregation in person, (2) offering pastoral/congregational care, (3) bringing a familiar sacrament to the person for the encouragement of their spirit, and (4) bringing that person's concerns or greetings back to the pastor and/or congregation.

1. Make an appointment to make sure (a) the person wants communion or a pastoral visit, (b) the time is convenient for them and they can be prepared for you, and (c) they can invite other family members or friends to join them. Make sure they feel free to accept or decline this visit. When you make the appointment,

make sure that there are no dietary restrictions. Let the coordinator know the particulars of your appointment by email.

2. Bring a communion set with you that should include the following: small pieces of bread or wafers (gluten-free if needed), a container of grape juice or wine (both previously blessed by the pastor), small cups, a plate, a white cloth or napkin, several communion booklets for liturgy (see next), a Bible, and hand sanitizer.
3. If possible, go with another trained communion visitor in order to more fully represent the congregation.
4. Begin with pastoral conversation (rather than just chitchat) about how the person is doing. Any concerns raised in this conversation can be reflected in the prayer following communion.
5. When you sense that it is time to begin celebrating communion, make the shift to worship clear and intentional by saying something like, "Shall we turn to a time of worship now?" If there are two ministers, one can prepare the elements while the conversation is going on and then can invite this shift when the table is ready.
6. Use the liturgy in the communion booklet so the care receiver can follow along and participate if possible. They might be invited to read one of the Scripture lessons, for example, or offer part of the prayer.
7. Watch for feelings during the communion (tears, heavy sighs, and the like), noting that to yourself, and return to it at the end of the communion time if that seems appropriate.
8. Make sure that when offering the bread, you don't use too big of a piece for a person who might have trouble swallowing.

9. Explain to the participants how you will be doing the communion—bread first, eaten together, and then the juice or wine. Participate together in communion.
10. Conclude the worship with a brief benediction. After a few moments of silence, return to gentle conversation. The silence might invite the person to reflect on what their experience of communion was like. If they don't fill the silence, you might ask if there's anything they want to reflect on.
11. Stay for a short while in conversation before leaving. Provide a copy of the communion liturgy booklet for them.
12. Practice strict confidentiality. Whatever is said during the visit can be shared only with the pastor, the coordinator, or the care ministry consultant. Nothing, even a general statement about the visit, can be shared with another congregant.
13. After the visit, send an email to the coordinator with a brief summary of the visit and how it went. If you have concerns or questions, also share those in your email.

A Liturgy for Home Communion

Invocation

Matthew 18:20 records that Jesus said, "For where two or three are gathered in my name, I am there among them." We gather now in Jesus's name.

Reading One: Psalm 23 (KJV)

The Lord is my shepherd; I shall not want.
He maketh me to lie down in green pastures: he leadeth me beside the still waters.
He restoreth my soul: he leadeth me in the paths of righteousness for his name's sake.
Yea, though I walk through the valley of the shadow of death, I will fear no evil: for thou art with me; thy rod and thy staff they comfort me.
Thou preparest a table before me in the presence of mine enemies: thou anointest my head with oil; my cup runneth over.
Surely goodness and mercy shall follow me all the days of my life: and I will dwell in the house of the Lord for ever.

Reading Two: Romans 8:35, 37–39 (RSV)

Who shall separate us from the love of Christ? Shall tribulation, or distress, or persecution, or famine, or nakedness, or peril, or sword? . . . No, in all these things we are more than conquerors through him who loved us. For I am sure that neither death, nor life, nor angels, nor principalities, nor things present, nor things to come, nor powers, nor height, nor depth, nor anything else in all creation, will be able to separate us from the love of God in Christ Jesus our Lord.

May God add a blessing to our hearing of the Word. Amen.

Prayer of Thanksgiving before Communion

Blessed are you, O God, who with your word and Holy Spirit created all things and called them good. In Jesus Christ your word became flesh and dwelt among us. Through Jesus's death and resurrection, you have destroyed the power of sin and death forever.

We thank you for the gift of communion, for the bonds of community and praise that we experience within it, which we share together today.

We give thanks that this bread and juice were prayed over by our pastor and congregation, that they prayed the words of institution and called forth your Holy Spirit to make them be for us the body and blood of Christ.

We take communion together now in the sure and certain hope that through this mysterious meal, we will receive anew and afresh the power of your spirit and our sense of oneness with you and with the community of Christ.

Through Christ, with Christ, and in Christ, in the unity of the Holy Spirit, all honor and glory are yours, O God, now and forever.

Amen.

Giving and Receiving the Bread and Juice or Wine

The bread of life, given for you.

The cup of the new covenant, given for you.

Closing Prayer

God, we give you thanks for the world you have created, for the gift of life, and for giving yourself to us in Jesus Christ. We thank you for the power of your Holy Spirit, who is always with us. We thank you for giving us this holy sacrament of communion, to nurture us and bind us together in community.

We pray that you continue to strengthen our spirits and encourage us through the ups and downs of our lives. We turn to you now, in silent prayer, as we name those people and circumstances we hold close in our hearts. (Silence.)

And now we pray together the prayer that Jesus inspired, saying,

Creator God, Who art in heaven
Hallowed be thy name.
Thy Kingdom come, Thy will be done,
On earth as it is in Heaven.
Give us this day our daily bread,
And forgive us our trespasses as we forgive those who
trespass against us.
And lead us not into temptation
but deliver us from evil.
For thine is the kingdom, and the power,
and the glory forever.
Amen.

Benediction

The grace of Jesus Christ and the love of God and the communion of the Holy Spirit be with us all. Amen.

A Ritual for Ending a Care Relationship

As we come to the end of our parish companion relationship and return to our ordinary and valuable congregational relationship, let us give thanks for the times we have spent together.

(Each shares one thing that they have especially appreciated about this time together.)

Shared Prayer (in Unison)

Thanks to you, O God, for giving us the joys of companionship and care. In our meetings together, we have shared stories of good times and difficult times, but in all times, we know that you are with us. We ask for your continued blessing in our lives as we move on from the special relationship that we have shared during these times of transition. Walk with us as our journeys continue to unfold and help us always remember your faithfulness and presence. Amen.

To one another (*in unison*),

May the road rise to meet you.
May the wind be always at your back.
May the sun shine warm upon your face
and rains fall soft upon your fields.
And may you always be held in the hollow of God's hand.
Amen.

Appendix E

Reading Resources

Pastoral Care Skills

Emma Justes. *Hearing beyond the Words*. Nashville: Abingdon, 2006.

Justes helps the reader understand the practice of deep listening and its grounding in hospitality. The introduction is especially helpful.

Alice Morgan. *What Is Narrative Therapy? An Easy-to-Read Introduction*. Adelaide, Australia: Dulwich Centre, 2000.

This text presents an accessible introduction to the ideas in which narrative therapy is grounded as well as a helpful description of its key practices.

Doug Purnell. *Conversation as Ministry: Stories and Strategies for Confident Caregiving*. Cleveland, OH: Pilgrim, 2003.

A powerful book about the art of pastoral conversation, it offers illustrations, strategies, and specific situations to help people develop attitudes and skills for this ministry art.

Jeanne Stevenson-Moessner. *A Primer in Pastoral Care*. Minneapolis: Fortress, 2005.

This text gives an overview of the key elements of offering pastoral care in an accessible format. Chapter 2 is especially helpful.

Grief Care

Kenneth Doka. *Grief Is a Journey: Finding Your Path through Loss*. New York: Atria, 2017.

Written primarily for grievers, the book looks at the diversity of the grief experience and offers perspectives for moving through it. It also looks at types of grief, including those that receive little social support for the mourners.

Melissa Kelly. *Grief: Contemporary Theory and the Practice of Ministry*. Minneapolis: Fortress, 2010.

This is a good summary of recent research and the practice of grief ministry.

Michael White. "Saying Hullo Again: The Incorporation of the Lost Relationship in the Resolution of Grief." In *Selected Papers*, edited by Michael White, 29–36. Adelaide, Australia: Dulwich Centre, 1989.

White presents the idea of helping grieving people reestablish a new relationship with their deceased loved one rather than trying to let them go and gain closure to the relationship.

Care with the Dying

Lorraine Hedtke. "Dancing with Death." *Gecko: A Journal of Deconstruction and Narrative Ideas in Practice* 2 (2000): 5–16. https://rememberingpractices.com/wp-content/uploads/2019/11/Dancing-Death-US.pdf.

Hedtke proposes three key ideas in working with dying people and their families: affirming the ongoingness of life and relationships rather than dwelling on the finality of death, appreciating how the emergency of death provides opportunities for the telling and performing of love stories that Hedtke hopes will linger long after the death, and asking questions to generate affirming and resourceful memories of this time and for future times of reflection and re-membering.

Lorraine Hedtke and John Winslade. *Re-membering Lives: Conversations with the Dying and the Bereaved*. New York: Routledge, 2016.

The authors explore ways to help people engage in constructive conversation with their loved ones during the dying process in order to facilitate a re-membering together. It also explores how bereaved people can create and maintain ongoing connections with someone who has died. A powerful, breakthrough book.

Care with People Who Experience Dementia

Colette Bachand-Wood. *Do This, Remembering Me: The Spiritual Care of Those with Alzheimer's and Dementia*. New York: Morehouse, 2016.

Through the telling of stories and ministry experiences, this author describes families and individuals living through dementia. She invites the reader to reflect on what it means to be present to folks in these circumstances and offers both wisdom and practices for ministry.

Eileen Shamy. *A Guide to the Spiritual Dimension of Care for People with Alzheimer's Disease and Related Dementia: More Than Body, Brain, and Breath*. Philadelphia: Jessica Kingsley, 2003.

Shamy focuses on the importance of living in the moment with people experiencing dementia, knowing that the positive feelings that occur during a pastoral visit stay with the care seeker even when the actual memory of the visit fades away. She also advocates taking a "what remains" perspective rather than "what has been lost" when offering care to people experiencing dementia.

God's Role in Tragic Times

Howard Stone and James Duke. *How to Think Theologically*. 3rd ed. Minneapolis: Fortress, 2013.

Stone and Duke invite the reader to recognize themselves as theologians. They then discuss the meanings of theology and theological reflection and explore the move from an embedded theology to a deliberative one. A good book for helping people begin to explore how they can intentionally reflect on their religious beliefs.

Jeffry Zurheide. *When Faith Is Tested: Pastoral Responses to Suffering and Tragic Death*. Minneapolis: Fortress, 1997.

Zurheide, who lost his own young son to death, explores the question, "How can a good God allow evil and tragedy to occur?" The first two chapters look at how a caregiver enters into a pastoral relationship in the midst of tragedy. The third chapter discusses ways people try to answer the theodicy question. A good book to generate discussion about how group members answer that question for themselves. See especially chapters 1, 2, and 3.

Appendix F

A Sampler of Stories from Members of a Care Companion Group

We end with some stories from people who have been care companions for several years and have participated in the same learning community together throughout that time. They have been helpful consultants for us as we have developed and written this book, and we are grateful to them for that. Here are their words.

J.

My time as a parish companion has been a unique and gratifying experience. I had the honor to be a companion to a retired clergy gentleman during his journey through the unfortunate stages of dementia. Because his situation was unusual, our time frame together was longer than normal. I was quickly able to decipher his favorite topics of conversation. They were his family, his faith, and his spirituality. We would have lively conversations, often repeating the same stories over and over. A most memorable experience for me was role reversal. I would perform the communion ritual, something he had done hundreds of times. Up until the final stages, when communication was difficult, there was one prayer that he never forgot. He could always recite the Lord's Prayer. I have come away from this experience knowing that life, no matter where it takes us, has meaning and purpose. We always ended our time together not with "Goodbye" but "To be continued."

G.

When I began as a parish companion, I was nervous about whether I could be helpful in my care relationship. I felt we had developed an open sharing connection, but it seemed our conversations stayed chatty and surface level. The active listening still felt awkward to me. I refocused my efforts on what I'd learned and did some practicing so that it would be more comfortable. Then in our next call, the care seeker told me, "Something happened last week, and I am so glad I can talk to you about it!" I listened reflectively as she talked and cried and made sense of her experience. It was then that I knew I was becoming a trusted partner, that she was really feeling listened to. I was offering something to her in a safe, sacred space. It was a meaningful moment when I could better understand what it meant to be a parish companion.

D.

A man I had been companioning lost his wife unexpectedly. He needed to grieve. What helped him was reading letters his wife had written to him, looking at his wife's artwork, and figuring out what to do with it. Going through his wife's art helped him find his way to happy memories. I helped him find his own way through active listening, and he helped himself by receiving his own words back, paraphrased into something that made sense to him.

S.

"Holy encounters that left a deep impression on me" might be a way I would describe my experience as a parish companion. Two years is longer than relationships are normally in place, but Covid-19 upended "normal," as we all know. My journey with a lovely and gracious care seeker carried us from her husband's move to a memory care facility until sometime after his memorial service after his death from Covid-19. I was blessed to be her companion as she navigated a new life for herself and lived through the pain of witnessing her husband's mental and physical decline and death and its aftermath. In reviewing my notes from this time, I find that each meeting in person or by phone was different, unique, and God filled.

When it came time to end my relationship, *full stop* were the almost painful but necessary words I needed to hear from my group to understand the importance of bringing the relationship to a timely conclusion. I am part of a wonderfully supportive and generous parish companion team who listened patiently and offered gentle yet astute observations. I hope I might do the same for them.

K.

The parish companions are a wonderful group of men and women who have a strong desire to help others who are experiencing difficult times. Our parish nurse and lead consultant saw something in each of us and invited us to be part of this new ministry. They believed it would benefit not only others but also us. Our group gives us the opportunity to learn in a variety of ways: educationally, highlighting important topics such as confidentiality, listening skills, boundaries, grief, and so on; experientially, role-playing to build skills (the most difficult for me); and through consulting, where we discuss our visits (confidentially) and exchange constructive feedback without criticism or shame. We are a cohesive and committed group, carefully tended by our leaders and by one another. The mutual trust and openness in our group lead to the success of our ministry.

NOTES

CHAPTER 2. PRESENTING NARRATIVE THERAPY THEORY

1 For further study of narrative therapy theory and practice, we recommend the following authors: Michael White, David Epston, Stephen Madigan, Jill Freedman, Gene Combs, John Winslade, and Gerald Monk. Current developments can be explored through the website https://dulwichcentre.com.au/ and through the *International Journal of Narrative Therapy and Community Work*.

2 Michael White and David Epston, *Narrative Means to Therapeutic Ends* (New York: W. W. Norton, 1990).

3 Christie Cozad Neuger, "Image and Imagination: Why Inclusive Language Matters," in *Engaging the Bible in a Gendered World*, ed. Linda Day and Carolyn Pressler (Louisville, KY: Westminster John Knox, 2006), 154.

4 Barbara Wingard and Jane Lester, *Telling Our Stories in Ways That Make Us Stronger* (Adelaide, South Australia: Dulwich Centre, 2001), v–vii.

5 Gene Combs and Jill Freedman, *Narrative Therapy: The Social Construction of Preferred Realities* (New York: Norton, 1996), chap. 2.

6 Alice Morgan, *What Is Narrative Therapy? An Easy-to-Read Introduction* (Adelaide, South Australia: Dulwich Centre, 2001), 55.

7 Stephen Madigan, "Counterviewing Injurious Speech Acts: Destablising Eight Conversational Habits of Highly Effective Problems," *International Journal of Narrative Therapy and Community Work*, no. 1 (2003): 52.

8 J. K. Rowling, *Harry Potter and the Sorcerer's Stone* (New York: Scholastic, 1998).

9 Stephen Madigan, *Narrative Family Therapy with Dr. Steve Madigan: Family Therapy with the Experts* (Boston: Allyn & Bacon, 1999), DVD.

Chapter 3. Narrative Practices for Lay Pastoral Care

1 Peggy Ann Ellingson, "Living in a Fish Bowl: Jesus Did It, So Can You" (unpublished manuscript), quoted in Jeanne Stevenson-Moessner, *A Primer in Pastoral Care* (Minneapolis: Fortress, 2005), 20–21.

2 Doug Purnell, *Conversation as Ministry* (Cleveland, OH: Pilgrim, 2003), chap. 3.

3 Emma Justes, *Hearing beyond the Words* (Nashville: Abingdon, 2006), xi.

4 Gerard Egan and Robert Reese, *The Skilled Helper*, 11th ed. (Boston: Cengage, 2018), 100–102.

5 White and Epston, *Narrative Means*, 38.

6 Cofounder of narrative therapy Michael White commonly used this phrase for alternative stories that hadn't been articulated.

7 Michael White, *Maps of Narrative Practice* (New York: W. W. Norton, 2007). The use of these kinds of questions is explained throughout this book as White sets forth a framework for doing narrative therapy.

Chapter 4. Collaborative Learning Communities

1 Harlene Anderson, "The Heart and Spirit of Collaborative Therapy: The Philosophical Stance—'a Way of Being' in Relationship and Conversation," in *Collaborative Therapy: Relationships and Conversations That Make a Difference*, ed. Harlene Anderson and Diane Gehart (New York: Taylor & Francis, 2007), 43.

2 See Anderson, 43–58.

3 Anderson, 44.

4 Anderson, 47.

5 Charlotte N. Gunawardena et al., "New Model, New Strategies: Instructional Design for Building Online Wisdom Communities," *Distance Education* 27, no. 2 (August 2006): 219.

6 Anderson, "Heart and Spirit," 52.

7 Sally St. George and Dan Wulff, "Collaborating as a Lifestyle," in Anderson and Gehart, *Collaborative Therapy*, 406.

8 Anderson, "Heart and Spirit," 17.

9 Jane Fried, *Of Education, Fishbowls, and Rabbit Holes: Rethinking Teaching and Liberal Education for an Interconnected World* (Sterling, VA: Stylus, 2016), 24.

10 Fried, xxvii.

11 Howard W. Stone and James O. Duke, *How to Think Theologically*, 3rd ed. (Minneapolis: Fortress, 2013).

12 While many texts bring insights into the questions of suffering and theodicy, one of the more helpful ones for lay pastoral care is Jeffry R. Zurheide, *When Faith Is Tested: Pastoral Responses to Suffering and Tragic Death* (Minneapolis: Fortress, 1997).

13 Ada Maria Isasi-Diaz, "Justice and Social Change," in *Dictionary of Feminist Theologies*, ed. Letty Russell and J. Shannon Clarkson (Louisville, KY: Westminster John Knox, 1996), 159–62.

14 Nancy J. Ramsay, "Analyzing and Engaging Asymmetries of Power: Intersectionality as a Resource for Practices of Care," in *Pastoral Theology and Care: Critical Trajectories in Theory and Practice*, ed. Nancy J. Ramsay (Chichester, UK: Wiley Blackwell), 166.

15 See Katherine Turpin, "Disrupting the Luxury of Despair: Justice and Peace Education in Contexts of Relative Privilege," *Teaching Theology and Religion* 11, no. 3 (2008): 141–52.

Chapter 5. Curricular Possibilities for Lay Care Groups

1 See appendixes for examples of these documents and other resources.

2 For example, see Lorraine Hedtke and John Winslade, *Re-membering Lives: Conversations with the Dying and the Bereaved* (New York: Routledge, 2017); and Dennis Klass, Phyllis R. Silverman, and Steven L. Nickman, eds., *Continuing Bonds: New Understandings of Grief* (New York: Routledge, 1996).